D1563044

J. S. Mill on Civilization and Barbarism

Also by Michael Levin

Marx, Engels and Liberal Democracy

*The Spectre of Democracy. The Rise of Modern Democracy
as Seen by Its Critics*

The Condition of England Question. Carlyle, Mill, Engels

J. S. Mill on Civilization and Barbarism

MICHAEL LEVIN

Senior Lecturer in Politics
University of London

 Routledge
Taylor & Francis Group

LONDON AND NEW YORK

First published 2004
by Routledge
11 New Fetter Lane, London EC4P 4EE

Simultaneously published in the USA and Canada
by Routledge
29 West 35th Street, New York, NY 10001

Routledge is an imprint of the Taylor & Francis Group

© 2004 Michael Levin

Typeset in Times New Roman by
Taylor & Francis Books Ltd

Printed and bound in Great Britain by
Antony Rowe Ltd, Chippenham, Wiltshire

British Library Cataloguing in Publication Data
Levin, Michael, 1940–
J.S. Mill on civilization and barbarism
1. Mill, John Stuart, 1806–1873 – Views on civilization
2. Civilization, Modern – 19th century 3. Civilization,
Modern – 18th century 4. Culture

Library of Congress Cataloging-in-Publication Data
Levin, Michael, 1940–
J.S. Mill on civilization and barbarism / Michael Levin.
p.cm.
Includes bibliographical references and index.
1. Civilization–Philosophy. 2. Mill, John Stuart, 1806–1873–Views on
civilization. 3. Mill, John Stuart, 1806–1873. On liberty I. Title.
CB19.L398 2004
901–dc22

2003055857

ISBN 0–714–65590–2 (hbk)
ISBN: 0–714–68476–7 (pbk)

Contents

'We have a warning example in China … they have become stationary –
have remained so for thousands of years.'

Acknowledgements

I am most grateful for the help and encouragement I have received from James Burns, Gregory Claeys, Janet Coleman, John Day, Clive Hill, Barbara Ballis Lal, Nirmala Rao and Georgios Varouxakis.

None of them, of course, bears any responsibility for the errors that remain.

Chronology

1806	20 May: John Stuart Mill born in London.
1809	First meeting of Bentham and James Mill.
1820–21	First visit to France.
1823	Starts employment at India House.
	Forms Utilitarian Society.
1826–27	'Mental crisis'.
1828	Promoted at India House.
1830	Meets Harriet Taylor.
1831–32	'Spirit of the Age'.
1832	Death of Bentham.
1835	Reviews first volume of Tocqueville's *Democracy in America*.
1836	Promoted at India House.
	Death of James Mill.
1838	'Bentham' essay.
1840	'Coleridge' essay and review of second volume of Tocqueville's *Democracy in America*.
1843	*A System of Logic*.
1845	'Claims of Labour'.
1846–47	Articles in *Morning Chronicle* on the Irish famine.
1848	*The Principles of Political Economy*.
1851	Marries Harriet Taylor.
1856	Promoted to Chief Examiner of India Correspondence.
1858	Retires from East India Company.

Death of Harriet Taylor Mill.

1859   *On Liberty.*

1861   *Considerations on Representative Government.*
Utilitarianism.

1865   Elected Liberal MP for Westminster.

'Auguste Comte and Positivism'.

1867   Proposes amendment to the Reform Bill to give votes for women.

1868   Loses seat in Parliament.

Retires to Avignon.

1869   *Subjection of Women.*

1870   Completes *Autobiography.*

1873   7 May: Dies at Avignon.

1879   'Chapters on Socialism' published.

Chapter One

Introduction

John Stuart Mill is remarkable not merely for the quality of his intellect but also for the breadth of his concerns. His writings cover the fields of philosophy, politics, economics, sociology, religion and psychology. This particular study derives from an initial interest in his political theory. Within that field scholarship has tended to concentrate around a few key issues. First there is the question of how Mill adapted his utilitarian heritage; of whether his suggested modifications reform or undermine it. Related to this is the question of whether *On Liberty*, his most famous work, is compatible with his professed utilitarianism or whether it is based on other principles. Second, there is Mill's attempted defence of individuality against both society and the state. This question involves the adequacy, or otherwise, of Mill's famous distinction between self- and other-regarding actions. Third, there is discussion of where, if anywhere, to draw the line on free expression. Fourth, in his *Autobiography* Mill declared his adherence to a 'qualified socialism', without saying precisely what the qualifications were. Fifth, the connection between Mill and liberalism has been much discussed, and is an issue to which I shall turn in the final chapter.

Here I shall suggest that the categories of relevance within which we place a thinker put the focus on certain issues concerning them and so necessarily downgrade or exclude others. In political theory we too easily ignore Mill's major contribution to economics. His *Principles of Political Economy* went through seven editions in his lifetime and was probably the major British economics textbook of the second half of the nineteenth century. Mill is also famous for the early and severe education that his father imposed upon him. He did not go out to school and so had minimal contact with other children. He was reading Greek and Latin at an age when other boys were sent outdoors to get some fresh air and exercise. His education, presumably, gave him his life-long commitment to education as such, and so he is well known for his concern with *individual* development.

What is relatively neglected, and what we shall here discuss, is that Mill showed an equal commitment to *societal* development and so can be placed in the discourse associated with such contemporaries as Comte and Tocqueville, with both of whom he corresponded, and with Marx, of whom he had almost certainly never heard. Like them he examined the mechanisms and the paths along which societies had developed from barbarism to civiliza- tion. For Mill personal and social development were parallel concerns. In both instances he looked for improvement. The individual has to be educated towards the higher pleasures, the society to civilization. The civilizing process, then, is necessary to both the individual and the society.

On the issue of Mill and civilization it is surprising how little interest there is in his belief that, at the height of its global power, Britain's civilization was coming to a standstill. It was the most serious charge that Mill ever made against his own society; not that you would know it from the secondary commentary.

FROM PHILOSOPHY TO POLITICS

One recent discussion of Mill's reputation states that 'Most commentators accord him a representative position in nineteenth-century Victorian liberal- ism.' Another describes him as 'the most celebrated liberal intellectual'.[1] A third notes that Mill's *On Liberty* 'is the most celebrated argument for liber- alism'.[2] As such *On Liberty* has stimulated a vast secondary literature dealing predominantly with the themes noted at the beginning of this chapter. This focus is on issues of principle that are both fundamental and probably timeless; hence the justification for concentrating on them. Margaret Canovan has noted that the 'meticulous study carried on by Mill scholars has been largely directed by philosophical concerns'.[3] Treating *On Liberty* primarily as a work of philosophy certainly has its justification in terms of the key issues raised. Furthermore, Mill's declared main purpose[4] supports this emphasis as, to an extent, does the nature of his own upbringing and life. Mill's *Autobiography*, for example, seems as much on the development of a mind as of a body, for he more frequently 'meets' and has better 'acquaintance' with books than with people.

There is also, however, a case for regarding *On Liberty* as a tract for the times and a contribution to the social debate of its day. These two aspects are, of course, not necessarily separate or incompatible, for eternal questions of principle can simultaneously relate to current political concerns. Furthermore, it is one of the characteristics and indeed one of the appeals of Mill's philo- sophy that by inclination he moves from theory to practice.[5] The relatively neglected final chapter of *On Liberty*, 'Applications', is one symptom of this. Indeed it was Mill's concern with social and political issues that often deter- mined which precise philosophical problems were given attention. Additionally, Mill the philosopher became Mill the MP for and at

Westminster. It is in the spirit of the breadth of Mill's concerns that we here turn from the philosophical and methodological aspects of *On Liberty* to the social purposes that underlie them.

In *On Liberty* Mill suggested or intimated, with varying degrees of explicitness and clarity, four separate reasons why liberty was necessary:

1. Individual liberty leads to the development of the faculties and capacities that are intrinsic and, to a significant extent, particular to each individual.

2. Individual liberty is a need of our human nature.

3. Liberty leads to truth.

4. Individual liberty is a prerequisite for the advancement of society.[6]

It is this fourth aspect that will be our concern here. This brings us to the fundamental political purpose of Mill's book: that he wrote *On Liberty* because liberty seemed under threat and, consequently, the very foundations of European pre-eminence were endangered. We have, then, two levels of concern that Mill was seeking to express: that of individual autonomy and that of social progress. The connection between the two was that only the former makes the latter possible. To an extent, then, liberty was a need of the individual nature; it was an end for each person[7] but simultaneously individual liberty was the means by which society itself advanced.

Our main purpose, then, is to work towards that aspect of *On Liberty* which consists of a social and political manifesto concerned to defend Western civilization against powerful tendencies eroding it from within. On this issue the example of China is crucial, for China is presented as a once advanced civilization that had come to a standstill, stuck in the sluggish backwaters of the historical stream. We shall trace the path that led Mill to this famous formulation in *On Liberty* and consider how coherent that formulation is, how it was viewed by his contemporaries, and the place it has in recent Mill scholarship.

John Stuart Mill's *On Liberty* was first planned in 1854 and published five years later. It was produced in a decade when the British were feeling particularly pleased with themselves. The Great Exhibition of 1851 signalled not merely relief at having escaped the turmoil that had engulfed many European powers a few years earlier but also a celebration of free trade and the global dominance of British industry. In the 1850s Britain produced over half the world output of coal and steel, about half the world output of pig iron and cotton and about a quarter of total world industrial output.[8] In 1859, the year in which *On Liberty* was published, Queen Victoria's speech opening the new session of Parliament included the following note of serenity: 'I am happy to think that, in the internal state of the country, there is nothing to excite

3

disquietude, and much to call for satisfaction and thankfulnesss ... a spirit of general contentment prevails.'[9]

Yet at the height of British power, one of its most celebrated thinkers doubted whether British or even European global ascendancy could be maintained. Mill clearly voiced his scepticism in one of the best-known political theory texts of his century; yet this aspect remained remarkably free from close scrutiny in the following one.

In terms of Mill's writings, our two main points of reference are his *Essay on Civilization* (1836), in which he first thoroughly outlined and discussed his understanding of the term, and *On Liberty* (1859), his most famous and enduring work of political theory, in which he questioned the durability of British civilization. We shall commence with a presentation of the former writing before turning to the cultural and personal background which facilitates our understanding of Mill's concern with this issue.

FROM THE BRITISH TO THE FRENCH

This is a study of Mill that is necessarily about more than Mill, for to understand him one needs to know his intellectual context, and that takes us into the utilitarianism of his family background, and such other influences as romanticism, Scottish political economy and the diverse products of French intellectual life. Mill, then, provides the focus of a debate on the meaning and consequences of civilization that we trace back some decades before his birth. It encompasses discourses on imperialism and orientalism, on Enlightenment optimism and conservative despair, on the need for leadership and the advance of democracy; in short, on the blessings, curses and dangers of modernization from approximately the time of the American and French revolutions to that of the so-called mid-Victorian calm in which *On Liberty* was written. We shall see Mill did not actually share the dominant complacency. *On Liberty* was just one contribution to a counter-cultural disquiet that believed modernization had sacrificed much of value and had created new dangers of its own. In working our way towards *On Liberty*, then, we shall confront the wider debate, mainly in Great Britain and France, on civilization and modernity themselves.

Mill's formative influence was clearly that of the utilitarian creed inculcated by his father in a chillingly thorough attempt at indoctrination. It is a heart-warming lesson on the failure of such efforts that Mill developed any independence of mind at all. At the age of thirteen he was sent for a year to France with the family of Samuel Bentham, the brother of the great philosopher of utilitarianism. Whatever John Stuart Mill imbibed of the family creed, the experience, without doubt, also set him on his life-long path of sympathetic engagement with French thought. Our precise topic, then, relates

4

both to Mill's placing in respect of the doctrine imposed on him and with his freely chosen intellectual relationships. It is, to some extent, a dialogue with the French.

The French, of course, had experienced the most dramatic recent history. The main home of the Enlightenment was also the land of revolution. The rationality of the former grappled with the task of integrating the irrationality of the latter. Was the great revolution of 1789 an unnatural diversion from normality, or was it part of the long-term pattern of development? Ann Robson notes that Mill 'read Auguste Comte's early *Système de politique positive* (1824) and learnt of the stages of historical development, the characteristics of an age of transition, and, most importantly, the significance for historical progress of the French Revolution'.[10] In his *Autobiography* Mill acknowledged the extent to which the French Revolution, and even an English reworking of it, had played upon his youthful imagination: 'I learnt, with astonishment, that the principles of democracy ... had borne all before them in France thirty years earlier ...What had happened so lately seemed as if it might easily happen again; and the most transcendent glory I was capable of conceiving was that of figuring, successful or unsuccessful, as a Girondist in an English convention.'[11]

This confession is further indication of Mill's desire not just to understand the world but to help change it. Ann Robson also notes that the 'Saint-Simonians had a fundamental influence on him. Through their eyes, Mill had seen the promised land.'[12] In this context we can understand Mill's very un-British initial enthusiasm for the French revolutions of 1830 and 1848 as well as his interest in current socialist experiments.

From the Scottish Adams, Ferguson and Smith, Mill could find a concern with the pattern of historical development, but by his own time he could plausibly conclude that French writers were 'the real harbingers of the dawn of historical science'.[13] Georgios Varouxakis has noted that Mill 'saw France as a laboratory of mankind in the realm of new ideas and movements in the same way as his compatriots (and most Continental observers) saw Britain as a laboratory in terms of industrial and economic development'.[14] In the writings of Comte Mill found an attempted scientific study of society as well as a theory of the stages of thought; in Saint-Simon the periodization of history into critical and organic periods; in Guizot a sense of the development of civilization and its causes; and in Tocqueville an account of the primacy of democracy in the historical process and of the rise of mass society. Both intellectually and politically France served as the yardstick by which British society could be judged and usually found wanting. In 1833 Mill wrote for the Saint-Simonian newspaper *Le Globe* on a theme that frequently exercised his mind: 'Comparison of the Tendencies of French and English Intellect'. His findings did not flatter his own country. The English, it seemed, 'have never had their political feelings called out by abstractions' and were not particularly given to theorizing. The suspicion that here Mill might have been implicitly but deliberately downgrading his utilitarian heritage is not reduced by his observation that any recommended benefit has to be argued on the basis of its immediate practical consequences rather than its elevated principles. In England anything suspected of being 'part of a *system*' would be linked with unacceptable 'Utopian schemes'. The French, in contrast, evidently united the speculative eminence of the Germans with the practical qualities of the English. In 'political philosophy, the initiative belongs to France at this moment' because of 'the far more elevated *terrain* on which the discussion is engaged'.[15] To Tocqueville he wrote: 'You know that I love the French', describing France as a country 'to which by tastes and predilections I am more attached than to my own'.[16] In 1844 Mill described 'the French mind' as 'the most active national mind in Europe at the present moment' and declared that 'the history of civilization in France *is* that of civilization in Europe'.[17] This repeats a claim made eighteen years earlier.[18] His view was not as one-sided as these extracts might suggest, however, for Mill cared little for Robespierre and Napoleons I and III.

From Scottish political economy as well as from French studies of the development of civilization, Mill found a sense of the historical process that Benthamism lacked. Utilitarianism was perhaps fundamentally a psychological creed. Its foundation was a theory of human nature compared with which differentials of time and place were unimportant. Whereas the theorists of progress were concerned to demonstrate from where our civilization had come, for Bentham such an effort was both methodologically unnecessary and politically subversive. He suspected that too close an interest in the past might produce a Burkean veneration for it.

Mill shared Bentham's distaste for feudal nostalgia, but not his dislike of history. Mill wanted to know how our society had emerged, and also wanted the study of the past to be methodologically rigorous and, consequently, reliable; yet his rationalism did not lead to determinism. He was less confident than Comte, Saint-Simon or even Tocqueville, let alone Marx, that there were laws of development leading to an ascertainable future. Mill's whole education was one which saw progress and mental cultivation as fundamental. His political purpose was to overcome partial interests and move towards the greatest happiness of the greatest number. Both his intellectual and emotional make-up led to the view that improvement was definitely possible. Yet, even so, there are ways in which Mill combined Enlightenment rationalism with the Romantic critique of it. This duality is basic to our whole topic.

FROM THE RADICALS TO THE CONSERVATIVES

Yet simultaneously with his radical hopes for the future, from Coleridge, Carlyle and Tocqueville among others, Mill became aware of Romantic and conservative influences. From these perspectives development was not an unmitigated good. It had its drawbacks. It threatened to produce a mass society that silted up the stream from which it had been nourished. The Chinese example, demonstrating that even a developed civilization could come to a standstill, fits with the conservative motif that modernization puts civilization under threat. In what follows we shall see that Mill combined a radical acceptance of progress with conservative doubts concerning its cultural cost and sustainability.

SUMMARY OF THE FOLLOWING CHAPTERS

In Chapter 2 we shall focus on Mill's discussion of civilization in the 1836 essay of that name, while also noting his treatment of that theme in other writings prior to the publication of *On Liberty* in 1859.

Chapter 3 puts civilization in its context by differentiating it from the barbarism that was seen to exist elsewhere. Basic to Mill's notion of barbarism, the 'other' that was not civilized like 'us', was his father's celebrated book on India as well as his attempts to justify imperialism.

Chapter 4 shows how civilization is conceptually linked to the idea of barbarism and how ideas of progress sought to outline a developmental sequence from barbarism to civilization.

Thus far barbarism has been safely distanced, either in remote countries or else in earlier time in our own. Even more threatening is the theme of Chapter 5, that civilized societies themselves are not secure. What threatened was less the resuscitation of primitive barbarism but rather an ossification that was the intrinsic product of civilization itself. Both Scottish political economy and Tocqueville's theory of mass society contained intimations that modernity created problems that it could not solve and that, therefore, optimistic, deterministic and monolinear theories of unalloyed progress were in need of considerable revision.

Chapter 6 deals with the example of China and the warning that even a great and developed civilization could come to a standstill unless it facilitated and guaranteed freedom of opinion. In his most pessimistic account of his own society, Mill believed that the battle for liberty, and hence the struggle for continued global leadership, was being lost. The situation could be rescued only by a vigorous counter-movement against all the dominant tendencies of the age.

In Chapter 7 we shall note that Mill's warning on mass society and the ossification of civilization was neither taken seriously by contemporary critics nor granted much attention or analysis by political theorists in our own time. Finally we shall consider the extent to which our discussion has affected Mill's standing as a pre-eminent advocate of liberalism.

NOTES

1. G. L. Williams, 'Changing Reputations and Interpretations in the History of Political Thought: J. S. Mill', *Politics*, 15 (3) (September 1995), p. 183; J. Belchem, *Popular Radicalism in 19th Century Britain* (Basingstoke: Macmillan, 1996), p. 116.
2. J. Day, 'John Stuart Mill: *On Liberty*', in M. Forsyth, M. Keens-Soper and J. Hoffman (eds), *The Political Classics. Hamilton to Mill* (Oxford: Oxford University Press, 1993), p. 204. Williams had earlier made the same point. 'Common to the host of interpretations of Mill's political thought is the centrality given to the essay *On Liberty* ... in all cases *On Liberty* is crucial to the argument.' Introduction to *John Stuart Mill on Politics and Society* (Glasgow: Harvester, 1976), p. 9.
3. M. Canovan, 'The Eloquence of John Stuart Mill', *History of Political Thought*, VIII (3) (Winter 1987), p. 505.
4. See J. S. Mill, *On Liberty* [1859] (Cambridge: Cambridge University Press, 1989), p. 13. In the attempt to be student/reader-friendly all further quotations from *On Liberty* will be from this easily available paperback edition.
5. 'His plans always have a practical bias.' J. M. Robson, *The Improvement of Mankind: The Social and Political Thought of John Stuart Mill* (London: Routledge and Kegan Paul, 1968), p. ix.
6. Although points 2 and 3 are not coherently presented in *On Liberty*, I think the case for both can be made.
7. This, however, raises important and – in my view – irresolvable problems of compatibility with the views that some peoples are not fit for liberty and that some appear not to want or value it.
8. See E. J. Hobsbawm, *Industry and Empire* (Harmondsworth: Penguin Books, 1960), diagrams 23, 24 and p. 134.
9. *Annual Register 1859* (London: Longman, 1860), p. 3.
10. *The Collected Works of John Stuart Mill*, henceforth MCW, 33 vols (Toronto: University of Toronto Press, 1963–91), XXII, p. xliv.
11. MCW, I, pp. 65, 67.
12. MCW, XXII, p. xliv.
13. MCW, XX, p. 226.
14. G. Varouxakis, *Mill on Nationality* (London: Routledge, 2002), p. 95 and see ch. 6 generally.
15. MCW, XXIII, pp. 445, 446.
16. MCW, XII, p. 309 and MCW, XIII, p. 536.
17. MCW, XX, pp. 220, 230.
18. Ibid., p. 18.

Chapter Two

Civilization

THE WESTERN SENSE OF CIVILIZATION

The term 'civilization' did not become common in English until the late eighteenth century. Raymond Williams mentions that in the seventeenth and eighteenth centuries 'Civility was often used ...where we would now expect civilization' and that in 1772 Boswell regretted that Dr Johnson 'would not admit *civilization*, but only *civility*' into the fourth edition of his celebrated Dictionary.[1] Nearly a century before that, however, John Locke 'counted the Civiliz'd part of Mankind' to be those 'who have made and multiplied positive Laws to determine Property'.[2] So for Locke civilization began when law, and hence the state, arose to defend the natural right to property. Jeremy Bentham, a century later, had escaped from the legal career that his father intended for him and placed the critique of English law at the core of his analysis. Yet even for him, as for many others, the identification of civilization with the rule of law remained. Bentham regarded 'the principal object of law' to be 'the care of security. That inestimable good, the distinctive index of civilization, is entirely the work of law. Without law there is no security; and, consequently, no abundance, and not even a certainty of subsistence.'[3] The term 'civilization' was also used to describe a people regarded as 'polished', 'refined' or 'improved'. Adam Smith referred to 'the improved and civilized part of the world'.[4] He mentioned 'a humane and polished people' as civilized and gave the examples of 'the French and the Italians, the two most polished nations upon the continent'. He also identified 'sensibility' as the characteristic most suitable 'in a very civilized society'.[5]

For Adam Ferguson, the terms 'civilized' and 'polished' were synonymous. Among their major characteristics were conventions on the laws of war 'devised to soften its rigours'. Civilized people had 'learned to make war under the stipulations of treaties and cartels, and trust to the faith of an enemy whose ruin we meditate'. Ferguson also mentioned 'the employing of force, only for the obtaining of justice, and for the preservation of national rights'.[6]

9

It seems that in France the concept of 'civilization' emerged at very much the same time as in Great Britain. Norbert Elias believed that the 'first literary evidence of the evolution of the verb *civiliser* into the concept *civilisation* is to be found ... in the work of the elder Mirabeau in the 1760s', although, as we shall see below, Rousseau was using the term a few years earlier. This Mirabeau, whose more famous son played an important role in the early stages of the French Revolution, explained that 'most people' would say that civilization was marked by 'softening of manners, urbanity, politeness, and a dissemination of knowledge such that propriety is established in place of laws of detail'.[7] By 1828 the historian François Guizot was confident that for 'a long period, and in many countries, the word *civilization* has been in use'.[8] In the 1850s Arthur de Gobineau summed up his view of civilization as 'a state of relative stability, where the mass of men try to satisfy their wants by peaceful means, and are refined in their conduct and intelligence'.[9]

Who, then, was regarded as civilized, and (the other side of the coin) who was not? – for the purpose of the term was to differentiate. According to Elias, in France at least the first differentiation was between the court and the mass. Gradually the manners of the court became the norm for the society. 'Concepts such as *politesse* or *civilité* had, before the concept *civilisation* was formed and established, practically the same function as the new concept: to express the self-image of the European upper class in relation to others whom its members considered simpler or more primitive.'[10] From that point the concept became a means of distinguishing between one society and others; demarcating those deemed less civilized and, therefore, inferior. The whole point of the term, at least from the eighteenth century onwards, was bound up with the Western view of itself as in advance of the rest of the world; that it had developed and others hadn't.

For Locke, the American Indian was taken to represent man in the state of nature, enjoying the benefits of the law of nature though without the security of civilization. In the same vein Hume wrote of the 'great superiority of civilized Europeans above barbarous Indians'.[11] For Rousseau also, Europe was the site of civilization. In his view 'Europe has been, if not longer, at least more constantly and highly civilized than the rest of the world.'[12] The same distinction was apparent a decade later, in 1766, when Boulanger declared that when 'the people of a savage race come to take on civilization, we must never set a term to the process by giving them fixed and irrevocable laws'.[13] So we see that civilization served the function of not only differentiating Europe from the rest of the globe but also of elevating it. Europe demonstrated the standard of civilization to which others should aspire. Difference might, indeed should, lead to the desire to emulate. This was the mentality that Bentham noted and condoned in the policy of Peter the Great of Russia. The latter's country lay astride the boundary of Europe. The manners of his people 'were rather Asiatic than European'. It was this that Peter sought to overcome. 'He used', said Bentham, 'all possible encouragements ... in order to introduce European dress and European spectacles, assemblies and arts. To lead his subjects to imitate the other nations of Europe was, in other words, to civilize them.'[14]

Adam Ferguson noted that the 'genius of political wisdom and civil arts appears to have chosen his seats in particular tracts of the earth, and to have selected his favourites in particular races of men'. Putting it more precisely, the Scot Ferguson magnanimously conceded that it was England which had 'carried the authority and government of law to a point of perfection, which they never before attained in the history of mankind'.[15] Ferguson's contemporary Edward Gibbon clearly shared the same view. He contemplated 'the gradual progress of society from the lowest ebb of primitive barbarism, to the full tide of modern civilization' and concluded that, 'Without indulging the fond prejudices of patriotic vanity, we may assume a conspicuous place among the inhabitants of the earth.'[16]

This view seemed even more self-evident to nineteenth-century Englishmen. In 1846 Lord Macaulay asserted that the English have become

> the greatest and most highly civilised people that ever the world saw, have spread their dominion over every quarter of the globe ... have created a maritime power which would annihilate in a quarter of an hour the navies of Tyre, Athens, Carthage, Venice, and Genoa together, have carried the science of healing, the means of locomotion and correspondence, every mechanical art, every manufacture, every thing that promotes the convenience of life, to a perfection which our ancestors would have thought magical ... the history of England is emphatically the history of progress.[17]

Unsurprisingly, this view was less acceptable on the other side of the Channel. François Guizot believed that it was France which 'has been the centre, the focus of European civilization'.[18]

A key function of the division of peoples into rude and barbarian on the one hand and civilized on the other was to designate the superiority of the latter. From superiority stemmed control and so we can understand why the term 'civilization' came into use in the period of the European discovery and gradual domination of much of the rest of the globe. Elias notes that in 1798, 'as Napoleon sets off for Egypt, he shouts to his troops: "Soldiers, you are undertaking a conquest with incalculable consequences for civilization"'.[19] Adam Ferguson was clear that civilization had always led to control: 'rude nations ... always yield to the superior arts, and the discipline of more civilized nations. Hence the Romans were able to over-run the provinces of Gaul, Germany, and Britain; and hence the Europeans have a growing ascendancy over the nations of Africa and America'. Ferguson noted that the 'torrid zone' had 'furnished few materials for history'. It had 'no where matured the more important projects of political wisdom, nor inspired the virtues which are connected with freedom, and required in the conduct of civil affairs'.[20] Here, like so many others, Ferguson was much influenced by Montesquieu's theory that the South suffered the disability of an enervating climate. In *The Spirit of the Laws* Montesquieu had explained:

> The heat of the climate can be so excessive that the body there will be absolutely without strength. So, prostration will pass even to the spirit; no curiosity, no noble enterprise, no generous sentiment; inclinations will all be passive there; laziness there will be happiness; most chastisements there will be less difficult to bear than the action of the soul, and servitude will be less intolerable than the strength of spirit necessary to guide one's own conduct.[21]

A comparable view was held by one of Mill's foremost admirers, Henry Thomas Buckle, the first volume of whose *History of Civilization in England* was published in 1857.[22] Buckle believed that the human mind had been able to develop only in those parts of the globe where the forces of nature were comparatively weak. 'It is accordingly in Europe alone, that man has really succeeded in taming the energies of nature', and where, consequently, 'every thing worthy of the name of civilization has originated'.[23] In Buckle's view climate determined food, which determined productivity, which determined the distribution of wealth. Civilization could develop only where the level of production facilitated the emergence of a class able to devote its time and energies to intellectual problems.

A normal feature of eighteenth- and nineteenth-century thought was that civilization was taken to be singular. This assumed a unilinear development in the direction of those societies presumed to be advanced. A plural definition, by contrast, takes Western, modern society to be one civilization among others. We shall see that Mill very occasionally referred to ancient cultures as civilizations, although his overwhelming tendency was towards the singular use. Raymond Williams notes that the first clear use of civilization in the plural was by Pierre Ballanche in 1819, but adds that this was 'not common anywhere until the 1860s'.[24] Among better-known thinkers we can mention Guizot, who in 1828 explicitly adopted a plural usage, instancing the Egyptians, Etruscans, Greeks, Romans and Indians.[25] A plural usage is also found with Arthur de Gobineau, whose *Essays on the Inequality of the Human Races* appeared between 1853 and 1855, that is just at the time when Mill first planned to write *On Liberty*. Gobineau outlined ten 'great human civilizations': Indian, Egyptian, Assyrian, Greek, Chinese, Italian, Germanic, and the 'three civilizations of America, the Alleghanian, the Mexican and the Peruvian', though he reduced any presumed cultural pluralism by deciding that they had all been 'produced upon the initiative of the white race'.[26]

The French historian who had most influence on Mill was François Guizot, whose *The History of Civilization in Europe*, the product of a series of widely acclaimed lectures, had been published in 1828, and was followed in the next four years by five volumes on the *History of Civilization in France*. This was only part of an intellectual output that would already have been more than a satisfactory life's product, but more than any of the other historians and philosophers who concern us in this study Guizot was at the centre of actual political power. He was the French Minister of Education, 1832–37. In 1840 he became French Ambassador to London, during which time Mill dined out with him. Later he became Foreign Minister and Prime Minister until the 1848 revolution ended his political career.

In April 1835 Mill wrote to the author and ex-cleric Joseph Blanco White: 'Did you ever read Guizot's lectures? If not, pray do.'[27] White did so, for his review of Guizot's lectures on European civilization appeared, with additions by Mill, in the *London Review* of January 1836.[28] This was just a few months before Mill's own essay on 'Civilization' was published. The aspect of Guizot's account that Mill particularly chose to emphasize was the notion that civilization was still in its infancy. This was repeated in Mill's fuller examination of 'Guizot's Essays and Lectures on History', published in the *Edinburgh Review* of October 1845.[29] In Guizot Mill found a discussion of pluralism and centralization and of those factors that favoured freedom and had rendered European civilization progressive and other societies stationary. Guizot argued that in Europe no one principle had ever been able to achieve total dominance. Its civilization, it seemed, had been uniquely diverse. Hence it had never stagnated. This seems to have been fortuitous, for no moral superiority is attributed to the Europeans themselves. What had separated and elevated European civilization from the rest of the world was the advantage of having God on their side. It was part of God's purpose that Europe be different, for 'European civilization has entered ... into the eternal plan, into the plan of Providence; it progresses according to the intentions of God. This is the rational account of its superiority.' It was a commonplace that change and development were hallmarks of civilization. Guizot remarked that the 'idea of progress, of development, appears to me the fundamental idea contained in the word, civilization'.[30] It was nearly as axiomatic that civilization was coterminous with Christendom. It seems that Mill and the utilitarians designated as civilized the very area that others simultaneously labelled as Christian. On the whole they preferred not to notice this alignment, although Mill, following both Guizot and Comte, did acknowledge the positive role of the Roman Catholic Church in the middle ages. The implication of the identification of Christianity with progress is the existence of a causal link; either theological, as with Guizot and his pupil Tocqueville, or secular, in terms of the propitiousness of the ethic of its Protestant sector with commercial or capitalist development, as later with Max Weber. Anyway, Guizot was one of a number of French writers who stimulated

Mill to consider how and from what Western civilization had advanced; and where, precisely, it had reached.

'THE SPIRIT OF THE AGE'

Mill's earliest treatment of our main theme occurs in works that have not received much scholarly attention. 'The Spirit of the Age' (1831) is not discussed in the introduction to its volume in Mill's *Collected Works*, volume XXII, while his 1836 essay on 'Civilization' is similarly neglected in what still remains the most recent full biography, Michael Packe's *John Stuart Mill* of 1954.[31]

Mill's five articles on 'The Spirit of the Age' were spread over seven issues of *The Examiner*, a journal edited by his friend Albany Fonblanque, between January and May of 1831. This was the first period of apparent progressive advance in Mill's lifetime. In France the restoration monarchy of Charles X had been overthrown. In the previous autumn Mill had rejoiced in 'the intense activity of a people which, freed from its shackles, will speedily outstrip all the rest of the world in the career of civilization'.[32] Within a month of the revolution breaking out Mill was in Paris to share in the excitement. In his *Autobiography* he recalled how the revolution in France of 1830 'roused my utmost enthusiasm, and gave me, as it were, a new existence'.[33] We see this already in the opening page of his first 'Spirit of the Age' article, where Mill imagined that his century would match the revolutionary achievements of the previous one. He took the belief as 'already not far from being universal, that the times are pregnant with change; and that the nineteenth century will be known to posterity as the era of one of the greatest revolutions of which history has preserved the remembrance'.[34] In his *Autobiography* Mill recalled that in the previous few years he had been particularly influenced by the writings of the Saint-Simonian school: 'I was greatly struck with the connected view, which they for the first time presented to me, of the natural order of human progress; and especially with their division of all human history into organic periods and critical periods.' It was clear to Mill that the main feature of his time was that of a critical period, an age of transition, 'in which mankind lose their old convictions without acquiring any new ones of a general or authoritative character, except the conviction that the old are false'.[35] This situation, he thought, had existed since 1789.[36] Mill thus sought to connect his own time with that of the most dramatic of all revolutions and his own country with that of France. He took French history as his beacon of the future, as his norm of development, as Tocqueville took America, and French thought as being the most progressive.

What, then, of Britain, the country that had remained constitutionally and socially intact during the revolutionary and Napoleonic epoch? Mill noted that 'almost every nation on the continent of Europe has achieved, or is in the course of rapidly achieving, a change in its form of government'.[37] It seemed that even Britain was capable of responding to this mood. The period of repression that went back to Peterloo, the 'Six Acts' and beyond was drawing to a close. The Test and Corporation Act had been repealed in 1828 and Catholic Emancipation was granted a year later. On 2 November 1830 the Duke of Wellington declared his opposition to parliamentary reform and was forced out of office two weeks later. He was succeeded by a Whig administration led by Earl Grey and committed to parliamentary reform. In March 1831 the first Reform Bill passed its second reading in the House of Commons. In the same month the third of Mill's 'Spirit of the Age' articles appeared.

In these articles Mill's sense of excitement and optimism shines through. Their main theme was that society was suffering the disabilities of a transitional state. The old ideas no longer carried conviction. The constituted authorities no longer commanded respect. Power was held by those unfit to exercise it. Authority and ability no longer coincided. 'The discredit into which old institutions and old doctrines have fallen' was 'perfectly deserved'.[38] Society had to change so that expertise was elevated to the superior position its merits deserved.

For our purposes it is noteworthy that progress from barbarism to civilization is taken as axiomatic. Mill could presume that his readers knew which societies fell into which category. It is only in passing that Highland clans are mentioned as belonging to the former and the United States of America to the latter. It was also clear to Mill that it was laudable to civilize barbarian peoples. In a brief piece that appeared in the same issue of *The Examiner* as his first 'Spirit of the Age' article, Mill declared that 'for the purposes of civilizing the Indians … the conduct of the United States towards the Indian tribes has been throughout, not only just, but noble'.[39]

Mill operated within a Saint-Simonian framework of transitional and constructive epochs which was assumed rather than fully delineated or explained. In so far as a theory of development can be discerned, it seems to be a 'tendency of civilization … to render some of those who are excluded from power, fitter and fitter for it, and on the other hand … to render the monopolizers of power, actually less fit for it than they were originally'. Mill noted the common view 'on the decline of the ancient commonwealths, that luxury deadens and enervates the mind' but further suggested that in his own time secure possession without exertion had led to the deterioration of 'the higher classes'. It seemed that 'for a considerable length of time in modern Europe … the qualification for power has been, and is, anything rather than fitness for it'. Gradually, 'through the advancement of civilization', others have gained greater fitness for rule than those actually in control 'until power, and fitness for power, have altogether ceased to correspond'.[40]

15

As Mill elaborates this view we see that it combines a number of familiar aspects of liberal theory: that unmerited power is to be condemned; that, in the words of the French Revolutionary axiom, careers ought to be open to talent; and that the educated and professional middle classes are more deserving leaders of society than the mere inheritors of aristocratic titles. All this is welded into a liberal theory of history according to which once merited power corrupts into its opposite.

What, then, was to be done? It seemed that sentiment in Britain was in advance of its institutional constraints and so our 'old institutions' needed to be 'made fit for civilized men'.[41] The Girondin Mill was keen to assure a British readership that radical reform could avoid Jacobin excesses. According to Michael Packe, James Mill's closest link with his 'favourite associates, Bentham, Brougham, Ricardo, M'Culloch, Grote and the others, was his dislike of violence'.[42] John Coleman has suggested that James Mill deliberately omitted the French Revolution from the syllabus of his son's early and extensive education. 'For Mill's teachers – his father and Jeremy Bentham – a revolution based on the notion of natural rights was founded on fallacious principles.'[43] The English radicals wanted a clean, peaceful, gradual and bloodless transformation: the Enlightenment followed by deposal of the aristocracy and rationalization of the law, but no repetition of the storming of the Bastille or the 'reign of terror'.

Here, then, France was not the model and even for John Stuart Mill the recent French contribution to the advance of civilization had not been entirely positive. In British culture the main bogeyman of French history was not Robespierre, who, though coldly bloodthirsty, had at least not primarily threatened British lives, but rather Napoleon, who had attempted invasion and seriously disrupted British trade with continental Europe. General Napoleon had first achieved power through a *coup d'état*, not exactly Mill's notion of how power should be gained nor of whom should be gaining it. In the last of his essays Mill referred to Napoleon's 'abortive attempt to uncivilize human nature'.[44] What Mill wanted was 'a moral and social revolution which shall, indeed, take away no men's lives or property, but which shall leave to no man one fraction of unearned distinction or unearned importance'.[45] It is noteworthy that at this stage Mill made no mention of unearned wealth. So, for all the rhetoric of revolution, the aristocracy were left not only with their necks but also with their inherited property, a much less radical position than the one Mill developed a decade later in his essay on 'Coleridge', his articles on Ireland and his book on *The Principles of Political Economy*.[46] At this stage the revolution Mill wanted seems to be one of status rather than power. The economic advantages of the aristocracy were to be left in place though their significance was somehow to be diminished. It is clearly an unsatisfactory and insufficiently explained amalgam but one from which Mill expected 'vast improvements in the social condition of man'.[47]

Though Mill advocated change and saw history as a pattern of improvement, he was aware that the nations of the earth did not advance simultaneously. Some cultures were progressive and some were stationary, or as he occasionally terms it, some were 'natural' and others 'transitional'.[48] As humanity was still at an early stage of its potential development, it was imperative that 'Worldly power must pass from the hands of the stationary part of mankind into those of the progressive part.' In some instances this dichotomy refers to different sections of the same nation; in others it divides one national culture from another. In the fifth essay Mill compared 'two great stationary communities – the Hindoos and the Turks' with 'one *progressive* society – but that, the greatest which had ever existed: Christendom in the middle ages'. This was quite a compliment coming from an agnostic! Mill believed that in the middle ages the Catholic clergy, who for long 'were the only members of the European community who could even read',[49] were the fittest people to exercise authority. This, however, was a temporary situation. From being the carriers of civilization the clergy gradually become its obstacle; a 'lamentably effectual ... instrument ... for restraining that expansion of the human intellect, which could not any longer consist with their ascendancy, or with the belief of the doctrines they taught'.[50]

So the Catholic clergy are granted their moment of glory, but ultimately civilization advances through their defeat. The aforementioned 'Hindoos' and Turks are meanwhile forgotten. They remain, presumably, stuck in the medieval situation where a monolithic religion possessed 'sufficient ascendancy, to subdue the minds of the possessors of worldly power'. In Mill's time European ascendancy was assumed by its major thinkers and so we do not learn explicitly on what it was based. We are here not told what or who constituted 'the more advanced communities of Europe' nor what shift in the balance of forces gave them the unique ability to overthrow religious orthodoxy and so facilitate free intellectual enquiry. For the less advanced countries, however, the development of civilization led to a countermovement 'back into barbarism'. There the 'germs of civilization to come were scorched up and destroyed' as the hierarchy saw vividly the threat it faced and did all in its power to resist. Such a situation is 'irretrievable except by foreign conquest'.[51] This, in isolation, might sound like a reference to the 'Hindoos', Turks or Chinese, but actually referred to Napoleonic France. Thus Mill implicitly endorsed the war Britain was fighting during the first decade of his life, even though its result was to strengthen conservative and restorative influences.

The spirit of these essays is undoubtedly Saint-Simonian and pre-Tocqueville. There is no explicit awareness that progess might be double-edged and contain intrinsic disadvantages. Although old elites, the Catholic clergy and the landed aristocracy, have to be replaced, Mill wants them succeeded by a new elite, what Packe has described as 'an enlightened despotism by a scientific *corps d'élite* who, being the rulers naturally in tune with the dynamic of the age, would inaugurate plenty, peace, and the religion of humanity'.[52] Although Mill described how initially appropriate leaders eventually become ever less suitable, he did not, at the theoretical level, ponder whether power and luxury might not also corrupt their successors. And yet in the few derogatory remarks on Napoleon we find an opening to Lord Acton's liberal maxim that all power corrupts and absolute power corrupts absolutely; as also that a revolution can ultimately destroy the liberty it had originally facilitated.

In Mill's essays on 'The Spirit of the Age' we find a number of themes that will continue to concern us: a theory of change, a notion of civilization, consideration of how it had once declined, and the idea of progressive and stationary classes or peoples. The antecedents of parts of *On Liberty* are clearly apparent. In terms of immediate influence, Thomas Carlyle was impressed, but otherwise, as Mill later confessed, 'these discussions were ill timed, and missed fire altogether'.[53] In the same spirit, Packe thought the essays contained 'laborious nonsense'[54] and Alan Ryan clearly endorses Mill's decision not to reprint them, particularly as 'the essay on "Civilization" five years later said all he wanted and said it more clearly'. It is to that essay that we shall now turn, but not before rejecting Ryan's belief that 'The Spirit of the Times' was not the 'real Mill'.[55] Our contention is that it is almost impossible to designate some part of Mill's writings as more really him than others. We share with Hegel the belief that 'the truth is the whole' and believe, in this instance, that the ideas of this early work help illuminate the development of Mill's mind on the issues that concern us.

ESSAY ON 'CIVILIZATION'

We have noted that Mill's 1836 essay on 'Civilization' was not considered worthy of attention by Mill's most recent major biographer. We are unable to replicate this neglect as it was Mill's only work explicitly devoted to our key term. He was ill when he wrote it. His father was undergoing his final illness, but Carlyle thought Mill's symptoms were caused by worries over the relationship with Harriet Taylor.[56] Mill's letters and other writings of the period give no explicit answer as to why he chose to develop this issue at just this point. However, some hopefully plausible conjectures are not hard to make. Mill had been studying three major French authors, Tocqueville, Guizot and Comte, who surveyed history in the broad sweep. In April of the previous year Mill began to read the just published first volume of Alexis de Tocqueville's *Democracy in America*, on which he commented in the *London Review* of October 1835.[57] Here Mill found an analysis that took the United States as the foremost example of the democracy that was predestined to develop throughout Christendom. As evidence Tocqueville noted a gradual process of incremental levelling through centuries of European history and concluded that its culmination in equality must be accepted as a providential fact. Tocqueville brought to his report on the United States a historical, sociological and even partially psychological understanding that Mill, and many after him, found quite compelling. Mill had met Tocqueville in the spring of 1835 and since then had been in correspondence with him. In 1828, while a junior magistrate at Versailles, Tocqueville had regularly attended weekly lectures in Paris given by François Guizot. In these lectures Guizot had explained how European societies had, since the fall of the Roman Empire, developed through from barbarism to feudalism, absolute monarchy and modern civilization. We have already noted how enthusiastically Mill had recommended Guizot. A few years later, in 1829 and 1830, Mill had first become acquainted with the Saint-Simonians. 'Among their publications' Mill found one which seemed 'far superior to the rest'. It was a work in which August Comte outlined his famous periodization of history into theological, metaphysical and positive epochs. Mill very much approved. 'This doctrine', he said, 'harmonized well with my existing notions, to which it seemed to give a scientific shape.'[58]

Mill commenced his essay on 'Civilization' by explaining that the term could be understood in two senses. First, there was the broader sense of improvement in general and, second, the narrower one: 'that kind of improvement only, which distinguishes a wealthy and powerful nation from savages or barbarians'.[59] The contrasts here are worth noting. If wealth and power are what particularly distinguish civilization, then we might assume the savage and barbarian conditions are marked by poverty and weakness. A further contrast within the second definition is that Mill wrote of a civilized 'nation' on the one side yet has no collective noun on the other. This is already indicative of a distinction Mill made: that man was originally pre-social and without any kind of collective identity. The ability to combine is itself a measure of the advance of civilization.

Of the two usages, Mill chose to deal with the second, narrower, sense of civilization. The convenience and significance of this is that it enabled him to use the term in a critical sense. Civilization, then, was not an unmitigated good but simply, for better or worse, a contrast with the barbarian condition. It had a number of clear differentiating characteristics. *First*, there is the difference of population density and its aggregation. 'Thus, a savage tribe consists of a handful of individuals, wandering or thinly scattered over a vast tract of country.' In contrast, 'a dense population ... dwelling in fixed habitations, and largely collected together in towns and villages, we term civilized'. Mill throughout contrasts civilization and barbarism as synonymous with mass and individual. He projected an asocial individualism back on to earlier stages. This contrasts with the earlier views of, for example, Voltaire,

19

Ferguson and Burke, for whom man was social by nature, and the later views of Marx and Durkheim, for whom individuality came not first but last and so was a late product of the social process. *Second*, there is the difference of economic development. Here Mill echoes Hobbes: 'In savage life there is no commerce, no manufactures, no agriculture, or next to none', while 'a country rich in the fruits of agriculture: commerce, and manufactures, we call civilized'. *Third*, and crucially, there is the issue of co-operation. Here Mill reiterated the eighteenth-century image of man in the state of nature, largely or even wholly isolated and, at best, only spasmodically able to co-operate with others. 'In savage communities,' says Mill, 'each person shifts for himself; except in war (and even then very imperfectly), we seldom see any joint operations carried on by the union of many: nor do savages, in general, find much pleasure in each other's society.' On the other hand, wherever 'we find human beings acting together for common purposes in large bodies, and enjoying the pleasures of social intercourse, we term them civilized'. Civilization, then, is marked by the gradually increased capacity for co-operation.

This leads on to Mill's *fourth* differentiating characteristic, that concerning the rule of law: 'In savage life there is little or no law, or administration of justice; no systematic employment of the collective strength of society, to protect individuals against injury from one another; every one trusts to his own strength or cunning, and where that fails, he is generally, without resource.' In contrast, a civilized people 'rely for their security mainly upon social arrangements, and renounce … the vindication of their interests … by their individual strength or courage'.[60] 'There is not', Mill concluded, 'a more accurate test of the progress of civilization than the progress of the power of co-operation.' Thus among other reasons for the advance of civilization over barbarism is that in war the former is always at an advantage. One lesson of history is that discipline and co-operation are always likely to prevail, even against superior numbers.

On this presentation, when Mill wrote about his own society he was self-evidently talking about a civilized one, for it had towns and cities, organized stable commerce, widespread co-operation and broad acceptance of the rule of law. Mill was explicit. 'These elements exist in modern Europe, and', in contrast with Guizot who placed France at the forefront, 'especially in Great Britain, in a more eminent degree, and in a state of more rapid progression, than at any other place or time.'[61] In an essay of the same year Mill referred to the 'four great nations' – England, France, Germany, the United States of America. Presumably they were at the forefront of civilization.[62] Of all of this Mill approves. His basic criterion of civilization, however, was not that it was a stage of unequivocal improvement but, rather, that it was a *contrast* with savagery and barbarism. Put this way, civilization can be found to have its discontents, disadvantages or even accompanying evils. To say that the 'present era is pre-eminently the era of civilization in the narrow sense' is to imply that it has failed to be so in the broader sense of '*human improvement in general*'. Thus, although Mill held 'that civilization is a good' there was, nevertheless, 'much even of the highest good, which civilization in this sense does not provide for, and some which it has a tendency (though that tendency may be counteracted) to impede'. We have here the germ of the criticism that was to lead to his advocacy of the stationary state in his *Principles of Political Economy* twelve years later. Beyond the narrower sense of the term, Mill told us that 'We do not regard the age as either equally advanced or equally progressive in many of the other kinds of improvement. In some it appears to us stationary, in some even retrograde.'[63] Unfortunately in this rather generalized overview, Mill did not specify the evidence he had in mind. What is clear, however, is that he did not now adopt the term 'civilization' for the conventional purpose of self-congratulation. Western society may have come far in terms of development but its progress had been at a cost.

Mill then turned to the theme that had concerned him in his 'Spirit of the Age' articles. Rapid social change had produced a loss of moorings. Society was now suffering the disabilities of the transitional state. Caught between periods of equilibrium, it could not stand still. The only way was forward. Because of 'the entire inapplicability of old rules to this new position ... many new rules, and new courses of action' would have to be adopted. Who, however, would lead the way? It could not be the traditional rulers of society. They were no longer fit for it. Their ideas were too inflexible and, anyway, their power base was eroding. Whether through dissipation, revolution or edict, the landed estates in England, France and Prussia were gradually breaking up. In approximate accord with Tocqueville's idea of the inexorable tendency to greater equality, Mill noted that 'as civilization advances, property and intelligence become thus widely diffused among the millions'.[64] What were once the attributes of the few now become the possessions of the many.

Still following Tocqueville, Mill envisaged the creation of a mass society to whom power passes as its facility for co-operation grows. Co-operation certainly represents one of the positive aspects of civilization. In respect of strength, courage and enterprise, 'savages' might be hardly inferior to civilized people, but, like the slave, they are 'incapable of acting in concert'. Over time the developing division of labour demonstrates the benefits of co-operation, which slowly becomes habitual. The process of civilization, then, is one in which property and intelligence are diffused and co-operation increases. This was first evident among the middle classes in manufacture, in industry and in the enormous extent to which business was 'now carried on by joint-stock companies'. As a result the 'country is covered with associations. There are societies for political, societies for religious, societies for philanthropic purposes.' 'The greatest novelty of all, however, is the spirit of combination which has grown up among the working classes.' As evidence

Mill mentioned the benefit societies and 'the more questionable Trades Unions'. He also noted the combined effect of newspapers and the railways in aggregating opinion at a national level. 'Both these facilities are on the increase, every one may see how rapidly; and they will enable the people on all decisive occasions to form a collective will, and render that collective will irresistible.'[65]

We here reach the turning point of Mill's essay, from where it is nearly all downhill to the end. 'The chief power in society is passing into the hands of the masses' and they seemed unqualified to exercise it beneficially. This new situation had to be squarely acknowledged for it was no chance product. It is 'by the natural growth of civilization' that power passes from individuals to masses, and the 'weight and importance of an individual, as compared with the mass, sink into greater and greater insignificance'. This change 'is the greatest ever recorded in social affairs; the most complete, the most fruitful in consequences, and the most irrevocable'.

Such a transformation in the character of society was bound to affect its politics and general power structure. For Mill the rise of public opinion and democracy were synonymous. He next asked how the traditional ruling class, so blessed with advantages, were going to adjust to their changed circumstances. In a manner reminiscent of, and probably derived from, Carlyle, he doubted their ability to 'correct' civilization's tendencies. Time and progress had rendered some improvements among them. They were less arrogant and bigoted than before but still showed 'no increase of shining ability, and a very marked decrease of vigour and energy'. Individual excellence was clearly not their most conspicuous feature. Furthermore – another strong echo of Carlyle – there had 'crept over the refined classes, over the whole class of gentlemen in England, a moral effeminacy, an inaptitude for every kind of struggle'.[66] This change was beneficial for sociability and manners but detrimental for the growth of the necessary leadership qualities. It seemed a characteristic of civilization that heroism declined, submerged along with character and individuality into the anonymous mass.

From the debilities of a class Mill turned to those of their political leadership in the Conservative Party. His analysis here takes on a particularly polemical edge as he doubts whether the Conservatives are using the time still at their disposal to adjust to the new situation; whether they are educating the masses to wield the power that is coming their way; whether they are preparing the two most prestigious universities for their educational responsibilities to society as a whole. 'The Church, professedly the other great instrument of national culture' had degenerated into a defender of dogma, but Tory politicians would not countenance change to an institution that served them so well. 'The Tories, those at least connected with parliament or office, do not aim at having good institutions, or even at preserving the present ones; their object is to profit by them while they exist.'[67]

From Mill's choice of the Conservative Party as the proper agency of elite education the reader might well presume one or both of the following; *first,* that the British Government was then, as so often, in Conservative hands. In actual fact the Liberal Party was in power, having won both elections since the First Reform Act of 1832, those of 1832 and 1835. Mill might, then, with more relevance, have asked the party that was actually governing to outline its response to the new situation. *Second,* Mill's account appears to presume a natural affinity between the aristocracy and the Conservative Party. This was anything but self-evident. For example, the principal figures of the ruling Liberal Government included *Lord* Melbourne as Prime Minister, *Viscount* Palmerston as Foreign Secretary and *Lord* John Russell as Home Secretary.

The whole essay is clearly still within the mental frame of demanding leadership from its traditional suppliers, for Mill's strictures against the upper class were much greater than those against the middle class. Whereas the energies of the higher classes seemed 'nearly extinct',[68] those of the middle classes had become narrowly focused on the pursuit of wealth. This, however, was more than a narrow class attribute; it was characteristic of civilization as a whole.

By this stage there is less sense of civilization as a long process of advancement and more of it as a current condition in need of remedy. The emphasis now was very much on its disadvantages. It seemed a mixed blessing with many intractable and irrevocable aspects. Was there, then, anything that could be done to modify such a comprehensive force? Here Mill was not pessimistic. There were certain advantages which civilization could not produce but which could still be fostered alongside it. To rescue the individual lost in the crowd, Mill called for greater combination. This, of course, was happening with the rise of trade unionism. The Grand National Consolidated Trades' Union had been formed just two years earlier, but Mill here was not thinking of the working class. Rather he instanced the class of small producers who were falling under the sway of large capital. He then turned to his own category and declared that the 'spirit of co-operation is most of all wanted among the intellectual classes and professions'.[69] Literature particularly concerned him in view of its vital role in forming the mind of the age. When only a few books were published, each gained the credit it deserved and received a proper evaluation. Now that a multitude of publications flooded the market, no one work could make the same impact as before and, as with individuals, so with books, quality was submerged and lost within the mass. Mill hoped that, somehow, the leading intellects would co-operate to guide the public towards works of real merit. He did not mention that this aspiration was already being met by just the kind of publication, the *London and Westminster Review,* that Mill himself edited and in which his article appeared. There was surely little to worry about in civilization if its negative consequences could be so easily overcome.

Mill closed his essay with one of his life-long themes, the need to improve education. Here his concern was with 'the regeneration of individual character among our lettered and opulent classes'.[70] He explicitly mentioned that he was at issue with both the admirers and the reformers of Oxford, Cambridge, Eton and Winchester. Two key faults had undermined the educational role of the universities. First they had become agencies of training for the professions rather than communities of free intellectual enquiry. Second – and one suspects this is where Mill really wanted to direct his onslaught – true open education had been thwarted by the ordinance of adherence to the 39 Articles of the Church of England.[71] In the same month in which the article was published, Mill had written to Joseph Blanco White: 'I quite agree with you as to the desirableness of striking more directly than we have hitherto done against the prevailing tendencies of English religion.'[72] Mill declared that when the purpose of education was that of instruction in a particular dogma, then the highest intellectual achievements become unattainable. It was precisely for this reason that Britain had produced fewer outstanding works of scholarship than had Germany and France. The universities, clearly, were not doing the job Mill wanted from them, that of 'strengthening the weak side of Civilization by the support of a higher Cultivation'. What was required would have been a very radical reform, that of 'putting an end to sectarian teaching altogether'.[73] Religion would still be taught, but in the same spirit in which all other subjects were approached, that of genuinely free enquiry into all sides of the question. Mill, then, had, at some length, shown his concern with regenerating the character of the higher classes by recommending secular non-dogmatic education in the traditional universities.

Thus far it might seem that Mill provided only fairly vague and moderate solutions to what he presented as fundamental problems. The last paragraph of the essay provides a sting in the tail, however, for Mill attacked the security that civilization provided for the upper classes. He called instead for a society in which merit rather than birth was the fundamental principle. This would, of course, have had the most radical consequences for the Britain of his time. It is not clear to what extent Mill realized this, for he declared it impossible to 'undo what civilization has done, and again stimulate the energy of the higher classes by insecurity of property'.[74] This was actually less impossible than Mill supposed, but anyway he did not here follow through the policy implications of his principle, for we might plausibly suggest that it would involve the removal of the Crown, the aristocracy and their power base in the House of Lords and also the severe limitation of inheritance. Mill had already been bold enough to attack the Church of England for its stranglehold on freethought and so might well have decided that he had gone far enough. He had been more specific in a letter to Tocqueville in the previous September, when noting that 'everybody is full of the necessity of an absolute reorganization of the House [of Lords]: & by this time next year everybody will be for abolishing it, (at least as a hereditary & aristocratic body) altogether'.[75]

The 'Spirit of the Age' essays and the article on 'Civilization' are divided by six years. Over this time a shift occurred in Mill's mood. The optimism of 1830–32 soon evaporated. Neither the radicals in England nor Louis Philippe in France had managed to bring about the improvements that Mill anticipated. The English radical MPs were too few in number to influence the Whig ministry and were disinclined to ally either with Conservative opposition within Parliament or the working class outside of it. In July 1834 Mill noted 'the attempts of Louis Philippe to pervert the laws for purposes of despotism and vengeance ... his grasping avarice reigns supreme over the destinies of a great nation'. Two months later the French parliamentary session closed, having 'been productive of nothing but taxes, and laws for the suppression of insurrections'.[76] Fresh elections brought no improvement, for the liberal opposition was reduced from about 140 to about 100 deputies. Thus Mill's essay on 'Civilization' was much less optimistic than its predecessor. There was more Tocqueville and less Saint-Simon. We are now told of the growth of mass society and that, in consequence, civilization can actually have disadvantages. This bleaker aspect, so crucial for our enquiry, was completely absent from the earlier work and thus undermines any attempt to treat 'Civilization' as merely a second and more thorough version of the earlier essays.

We are, it will be recalled, tracing the path towards Mill's famous prognosis on civilization in Chapter Three of *On Liberty*. In that respect it is clear that the essay on 'Civilization' can plausibly be read as an early draft: for we have seen Mill outline the move to greater equality; the rise of mass society and its danger to the progress of civilization; the importance of associations; the significance of increased means of communication (the railways and the press); the decline of individuality and the concern with freedom of thought. In contrast, though, we still have here the notion that civilization's evils can be counteracted by a regenerated higher class. In this there is a temporary affinity with Carlyle as well as the more durable one with Coleridge's idea of a clerisy. In time it became clear that their respective elites were of a very contrasting type. Mill's essay had ended with a rather parochial focus. He began with an overview of broad historical tendencies and closed with a polemic against British elite institutions. It was a move from social theory to current party politics.

'BENTHAM' AND 'COLERIDGE'

For our present purposes we might here mention the essays Mill published on 'Bentham' in 1838 and 'Coleridge' two years later. Mill had personally met both men, but now took them less as corporeal figures than as representatives of certain clusters of ideas. Bentham was used as a symbol of the eighteenth-century Enlightenment and Coleridge as one of the nineteenth-century reaction to it. Mill had been educated as a disciple of the former but had become increasingly open to the ideas of the latter. It is perhaps not too cryptic or simplistic to suggest that the tension within his social and political thought results from the attempt to find a *modus vivendi* between two such antithetical outlooks. In each essay Mill presented a view of civilization consonant with the mentality of the particular thinker he was discussing. In the 'Bentham' essay his few comments were more in line with the articles of 1830: that in England there had been a long period of struggle between 'the old barbarism and the new civilization'. In so far as – a Benthamite touch – the 'basis of the English law was, and still is, the feudal system', the battle was still continuing. Mill sounded happy enough, however, with the current situation, for the 'armed encampment of barbarous warriors' had been converted into 'an industrious, commercial, rich and free people'.[77]

The 'Coleridge' essay, in contrast, shows much greater awareness of the costs as well as the benefits of civilization. For Mill now it seemed to be an open 'question how far mankind have gained by civilization'. He could well have been contrasting Bentham and Coleridge on this issue when he declared:

> One observer is forcibly struck by the multiplication of physical comforts; the advancement and diffusion of knowledge; the decay of superstition; the faculties of mutual intercourse; the softening of manners; the decline of war and personal conflict; the progressive limitation of the tyranny of the strong over the weak; the great works accomplished throughout the globe by the co-operation of multitudes.
>
> Another fixes his attention, not upon the value of these advantages, but upon the high price which is paid for them; the relaxation of individual energy and courage; the loss of proud and self-relying independence; the slavery of so large a portion of mankind to artificial wants; their effeminate shrinking from even the shadow of pain ... and absence of any marked individuality, in their characters; the contrast between the narrow mechanical understanding, produced by a life spent in executing by fixed rules a fixed task, and the varied powers of the man of the woods, whose subsistence and safety depend at each instant upon his capacity of extemporarily adapting means to ends; the demoralizing effect of great inequalities in wealth and social rank; and the sufferings of the great mass of the people of civilized countries, whose wants are scarcely better provided for than those of the savage, while they are bound by a thousand fetters in lieu of the freedom and excitement which are his compensations. One who attends to these things, and to these exclusively, will be apt to infer that savage life is preferable to civilized; that the work of civilization should as far as possible be undone; and from the premises of Rousseau, he will not improbably be led to the practical conclusions of Rousseau's disciple, Robespierre.[78]

This is a remarkable passage, fully worth the length I have allowed it. Mill was putting two sides of an argument rather than his own view, but it might be significant that he had more to say for the case against civilization than the one for it. That case, like its opposite, was taken as true but only part of the truth. It seemed to be a part, however, that Mill had fully integrated. We have here one of his few references to Rousseau and certainly many of Rousseau's main themes are echoed.

As a constant advocate of education, Mill is unlikely to have cared overmuch for Rousseau's *Discourse on the Arts and Sciences*, with its praise of 'happy ignorance' and its condemnation of 'useless knowledge' and 'vain sciences'.[79] Rousseau's *Discourse*, however, also foreshadowed Mill's basic theme of mass society, as we shall see in the third section of Chapter 5 .

The link with Robespierre seems gratuitously defamatory; an indication of the depth of feeling that Mill still had against those who had destroyed the more constitutional path of reform. Mill, after all, can hardly have seen Robespierre as an opponent of modern civilization who wanted to replace it with egalitarian, pastoral simplicity. Such was Rousseau's public image in spite of his belief that there was no going back to earlier conditions. Mill here falls into the Conservative mindset which since Burke had blamed the French Revolution on Rousseau and the Enlightenment, even though in 1837 he had favourably reviewed Carlyle's history of the revolution, where the responsibility was squarely placed on a negligent aristocracy.[80]

Although Rousseau hardly ever even makes the index of any book by or on Mill, Chapter Two of *On Liberty* contains what is on balance a flattering presentation of his ideas and one closely associated with our theme here. Mill believed that Rousseau furthered the cause of diversity by combating the dominant view of his day, which both over-praised current achievements and exaggerated the superiority achieved over their ancestors. 'With what a salutary shock did the paradoxes of Rousseau explode like bombshells in the midst, dislocating the compact mass of one-sided opinion.' This in itself would have been a service for liberty. Mill went further, however, stating that Rousseau's opinions on the 'superior worth of simplicity of life' and the 'hypocrisies of artificial society'[81] were actually nearer to the truth than were the views of his critics. In what might quite plausibly be a self-conscious though indirect critique of Bentham's worldview, Rousseau is singled out as the first critic of Enlightenment optimism. He could, thus, be placed on both sides; as opposed to the Enlightenment that allegedly caused the revolution but yet simultaneously a progenitor of that revolution.

In the next chapter we shall return to broader issues and turn back in time to consider from where civilization had come and with what it could, consequently, be contrasted.

NOTES

1. R.Williams, *Keywords: A Vocabulary of Culture and Society* (Glasgow: Fontana, 1976), p. 48.
2. J. Locke, *Two Treatises of Government*, ed. P. Laslett (New York: Mentor, 1965), para. 30, p. 331.
3. J. Bentham, *The Theory of Legislation* (London: Kegan Paul, n.d.), p. 109.
4. *The Wealth of Nations* [1776] (Harmondsworth: Penguin Books, 1973), p. 503.
5. *The Theory of Moral Sentiments* [1759] (Indianapolis, IN: Liberty Fund, 1984), pp. 207, 209. Thus we can understand how, in a usage most developed in Germany, civilization was identified with the culture of the court and the artificialities of courtesy. See N. Elias, *The Civilizing Process*, vol. 1, *The History of Manners* (Oxford: Blackwell, 1978), ch.1, esp. p. 9.
6. A. Ferguson, *An Essay on the History of Civil Society* [1767] (Cambridge: Cambridge University Press, 1995), p. 190. In the Introduction (p. xxii), Fania Oz-Salzburger states: 'The very first passage of the book features the word "civilization" in one of its earliest occurrences.'
7. Elias, *The Civilizing Process*, vol. 1, p. 38. See pp. 46–7 for Elias's view that the concept became 'widely used' in the 1770s. He also explains that civilization had a widely different meaning in Germany from that in France and Great Britain. See ibid., ch. 1, part 1. I have omitted discussion of the German usage as it was British and French thought which provided the frame of reference for Mill's own ideas.
8. F. Guizot, *The History of Civilization in Europe* [1828] (Harmondsworth: Penguin Books, 1997), p. 14.
9. Gobineau, *Selected Political Writings*, ed. M. D. Biddis (London: Cape, 1970), p. 91.
10. Elias, *The Civilizing Process*, p. 39.
11. D. Hume, *Enquiries Concerning the Human Understanding and Concerning the Principles of Morals* [1751] (Oxford: Clarendon Press, 1966), p. 191.
12. J. J. Rousseau, 'Discourse on Inequality' [1754] in *The Social Contract. Discourses*, ed. G. D. H. Cole (London: Dent, 1961), p. 199.
13. Quoted in P. Hazard, *European Thought in the Eighteenth Century* (Harmondsworth: Penguin Books, 1965), p. 397.
14. J. Bentham, *The Theory of Legislation*, p. 378. Another and fuller instance of accepting Europe as the norm for civilization is provided by a contemporary of Mill. See Domingo Sarmiento, *Life in the Argentine Republic in the Days of the Tyrants; or Civilization and Barbarism* [1845] (New York: Hafner, n.d.).
15. Ferguson, *Essay*, pp. 106, 159.
16. E. Gibbon quoted in R. Porter, *Enlightenment. Britain and the Creation of the Modern World* (Harmondsworth: Penguin Books, 2001), pp. 231–2.
17. Quoted in W. E. Houghton, *The Victorian Frame of Mind, 1830–1870* (New Haven, CT: Yale University Press, 1985), p. 39.
18. Guizot, *History*, p. 11.
19. Elias, *The Civilizing Process*, pp. 49–50.
20. Ferguson, *History*, pp. 93–4, 108.
21. *The Spirit of the Laws* [1748] (Cambridge: Cambridge University Press, 1989), p. 234. For the influence of Montesquieu on Ferguson see Introduction to Ferguson, *Essay*,

pp. xiii–xiv.

22. Buckle referred to Mill as 'one of the greatest thinkers of his time'. *History of Civilization in England* (London: Parker, 1861), vol. 1, p. 37. After Buckle's death in 1862, Helen Taylor, at Mill's suggestion, began work on the publication of his further writings.
23. Buckle, *History of Civilization*, pp. 140, 74.
24. R. Williams, *Keywords*, p. 50.
25. See Guizot, *History of Civilization*, pp. 28–9.
26. Gobineau, *Selected Political Writings*, pp. 142–3.
27. MCW, XII, p. 259.
28. See MCW, XX, pp. 367–93.
29. See Guizot, *History* p. 24 and MCW, XX, pp. 257–94.
30. F. Guizot, *History*, pp. 16, 32.
31. M. St. J. Packe, *The Life of John Stuart Mill* (London: Secker and Warburg, 1954).
32. MCW, XXII, p. 134.
33. MCW, I, p. 179.
34. MCW, XXII, p.228.
35. MCW, I, p. 171.
36. See MCW, XXII, pp. 292.
37. Ibid., p. 230.
38. Ibid., p. 231.
39. Ibid., pp. 245, 236.
40. Ibid., pp. 255, 279.
41. Ibid., p. 230.
42. Packe, *Mill* (London: Secker and Warburg, 1954), p. 101.
43. J. Coleman, 'John Stuart Mill on the French Revolution', *History of Political Thought*, IV(1) Spring 1983, pp. 89–110; quote p. 91. See ibid., pp. 105–6 for Mill's brief revolutionary enthusiasm some months after the 'Spirit of the Age' articles had been published.
44. Also 'a man in whom all the evil influences of his age were concentrated with an intensity and energy truly terrific'. MCW, XXII, p. 307.
45. Ibid., p. 245.
46. See M. Levin, The *Condition of England Question: Carlyle, Mill, Engels* (Basingstoke: Macmillan, 1998), pp. 78–9, 93–5, 98.
47. MCW, XXII, p. 241.
48. See, for example, ibid., pp. 291, 304.
49. Ibid., pp. 245, 305.
50. Ibid., p. 306. Mill forwarded the same view in his review of 'Michelet's History of France' in 1844. See MCW, XX, pp. 239–41.
51. MCW, XXII, pp. 305, 306, 307.
52. Packe, *Mill*, p. 98.
53. MCW, I, p. 181.
54. Packe, *Mill*, p. 98.
55. A. Ryan, *J. S. Mill* (London: Routledge and Kegan Paul, 1974), p. 41.
56. See Packe, *Mill*, pp. 204–8.
57. See MCW, XVIII, pp. 47–90.
58. MCW, I, p. 173.

59. MCW, XVIII, p. 119.
60. Ibid., p. 120.
61. MCW, XVIII, pp. 120–1.
62. From 'State of Society in America', MCW, XVIII, p. 94.
63. MCW, XVIII, p. 119.
64. Ibid., pp. 119–20, 122.
65. Ibid., pp. 125, 172.
66. Ibid., pp. 126, 131.
67. Ibid., p. 128.
68. Ibid., p. 130.
69. Ibid., p. 136.
70. Ibid., p. 138.
71. It is an extraordinary thought that, with all his intellectual prowess, John Stuart Mill, as an agnostic, was disqualified from entrance to Oxford and Cambridge universities.
72. MCW, XII, p. 301.
73. MCW, XVIII, p. 144.
74. Ibid., p. 147.
75. MCW, XII, p. 272.
76. MCW, XXIII, pp. 700, 702, 732.
77. MCW, X, p. 101.
78. Ibid., p. 123.
79. *The Social Contract. Discourses*, pp. 125, 126, 127.
80. See MCW, XX, pp. 131–66.
81. J. S. Mill, *On Liberty*, ed. S. Collini (Cambridge: Cambridge University Press, 1989), p. 48.

Chapter Three

Barbarism and the Imperial Remedy

BARBARISM AND SAVAGERY

All definition implies exclusion, for a definition is a statement of the limits within which a word will be used. The word, then, is meaningful only as a delineated differentiation from that which it is not. In the case of civilization, the most meaningful other with which it is contrasted is barbarism. The word 'barbarism' itself, of course, comes from the ancient Greeks, for whom it designated one who spoke another language. In this sense it might appear as a neutral term, but historically it has been quite normal for any one people to assume its own superiority over all others with whom it came into contact. For the Greeks, people who spoke other tongues were inferior. Adam Ferguson noted that among the Greeks barbarian 'became a term of indiscriminate contempt and aversion'.[1]   According to the Greek use of the term, barbarism was a fixed essence of the other. This usage survived into much later times. For example for Montesquieu civilization was determined by climate, morals improving as one nears the pole and declining towards the equator:

> You will find in the northern climates peoples who have few vices, enough virtues, and much sincerity and frankness. As you move toward the countries of the south, you will believe you have moved away from morality itself: the liveliest passions will increase crime; each will seek to take from others all the advantages that can favor these same passions.[2]

Strongly under Montesquieu's influence, Ferguson noted that the 'torrid zone … has no where matured the more important projects of political wisdom, nor inspired the virtues which are connected with freedom, and required in the conduct of civil affairs'.[3]

   Closely associated with barbarism is the idea of savagery. In the eighteenth century these terms were sometimes used synonymously[4] and at other times developmentally. Thus for Montesquieu one 'difference between savage peoples and barbarian peoples is that the former are small scattered nations which, for certain particular reasons, cannot unite', whereas barbarians are ordinarily small nations that can unite together. The former are usually hunting peoples; the latter, pastoral peoples.'[5] Similarly Adam Ferguson noted that savages survive on 'hunting, fishing, or the natural produce of the soil' and have little idea of 'property, and scarcely any beginnings of subordination or government'. Barbarians, in contrast, own and cultivate cattle and 'know what it is to be poor and rich. They know the relations of patron and client, of servant and master, and suffer themselves to be classed according to their measures of wealth.' The savage 'is not yet acquainted with property'; the barbarian, in contrast, has possessions but, as in Locke's state of nature, holds them without the security of settled laws.[6] Otherwise Ferguson found in the barbarian rather contrasting, if not contradictory, attributes. On the one hand 'the barbarian spends every moment of relaxation in the indulgence of sloth' and is often weak, timid and servile; yet, simultaneously endures an almost permanent state of war.[7]

For Jeremy Bentham, at least in his *Theory of Legislation*, savagery and barbarism seem identical. The condition was one of poverty, cruelty and vice. Once basic necessities had been attained, lethargy soon took over. 'The pursuit of revenge; the pleasure of drunkenness if he has the means; sleep; or perfect indolence; such is the sum total of his resources.'[8]

John Stuart Mill often wrote in a similar way, suggesting that among 'a timid and spiritless race, like the inhabitants of the vast plains of tropical countries, passive obedience may be of natural growth'.[9] The view that 'backward' societies suffered particularly from the lack of 'the effective desire of accumulation' was evidently more than confirmed by the efforts of the Jesuits 'to civilize the Indians of Paraguay ... The real difficulty was the improvidence of the people; their inability to think for the future: and the necessity accordingly of the most unremitting and minute superintendence on the part of their instructors.'[10] Mill sometimes followed Smith and Bentham in using the terms savage and barbarian as identical but at other times, as in the essay on 'Coleridge', he was with Montesquieu and Ferguson in distinguishing between the barbarian Germans and the 'still more unmitigated savages, the wild Indians',[11] thus clearly intimating that the former were a stage above the latter. The 'wild Indians' were clearly those of North America. In contrast, Mill often referred to the inhabitants of India as 'semi-barbarians'. Mill, like his father, never left Europe and for both of them the only direct and continuous interest they had for less developed societies was for the people of India. That relationship will be our main concern for the rest of this chapter.

JAMES MILL'S *HISTORY OF BRITISH INDIA*

There are many ways in which an author could introduce himself to his readers. Identification could be summarized in terms of beliefs, national or ethnic group, occupation or social class. In the second paragraph of his *Autobiography*, in what is the very first sentence of self-description, John Stuart Mill chose to describe himself as 'the eldest son of James Mill, the author of the *History of British India*'.[12] This is a significantly partial designation. He was equally the eldest son of his mother, Mrs Harriet Mill, or Mrs James Mill as Packe's index denotes her, but the maternal link was not relevant to the intellectual development that Mill wanted to describe.[13] Mill, then, chose to classify himself as an appendage of his father, which is certainly what James Mill intended to produce. Equally probably, the classification presented the educated public with a positioning in terms of a work with which they were familiar. It is not, however, obviously the work with which they were *most* familiar. In his 1992 Preface to James Mill's *Political Writings*, Terence Ball describes the *Essay on Government* as the work for which James Mill was best known.[14] There was, then, a choice of works with which John Stuart could plausibly have chosen to align himself. He could alternatively have identified his father as a major advocate of utilitarianism. So the son made his choice, and long after he had written critical pieces on his father's utilitarian beliefs, he apparently still endorsed James Mill's longest work, the six-volume *History of British India*. In 1865 Mill referred to his father as 'the historian who first threw the light of reason on Hindoo society'.[15] In his *Autobiography* Mill described the *History* as a 'book which contributed largely to my education, in the best sense of the term'. His father began writing *The History of British India* in the year his eldest son was born, so, in a way, John Stuart Mill grew up with it and it is certainly from there that he received an early impression of how a different culture was to be evaluated.

The *History* was published in 1818, the year of Mill's twelfth birthday. He had read the manuscript while his father corrected the proofs. Years later he remained enthusiastic about its formative influence:

> The number of new ideas which I received from this remarkable book, and the impulse and stimulus as well as guidance given to my thoughts by its criticisms and disquisitions on society and civilization in the Hindoo part, on institutions and the acts of governments in the English part, made my early familiarity with it eminently useful to my subsequent progress.[16]

It was largely on the strength of his *History of British India* that in 1819 James Mill was appointed an Assistant Examiner for the British East India Company. He remained with the company until his death in 1836, having become Chief Examiner in 1830, 'a virtual Under-Secretary of State for India', according to one account.[17]

The East India Company was a commercial enterprise which in 1600 received a charter from Queen Elizabeth I allowing it certain trading privileges. Military force proved necessary to defend its position and so, in time, a nominally private commercial company developed governmental functions, gradually expanding its area of control and taking over, at great profit to itself, the administration of taxes and justice in the regions it dominated. In 1813, however, the company lost its trading monopoly and in 1834 gave up all commercial functions. In 1823, at the age of seventeen, John Stuart Mill followed his father into the East India Company, as he had earlier followed him into utilitarianism. He performed the job to the evident satisfaction of his superiors, being first promoted in 1828, then again in 1836 and finally in 1856 attaining the post previously held by his father, that of Chief Examiner of India Correspondence. A year later the Indian Mutiny broke out, after which Parliament took over the direct administration of the company's territory. Mill strongly opposed this, believing that a detrimental conflict of interest would occur when decisions on India were taken by politicians mainly concerned to appease their home electorate. He thus chose to go into retirement rather than accept the post he was offered in the new administration of India. Mill had been at the India Office for thirty-five years. It was his only full-time job apart from his three years as Member of Parliament for Westminster from 1865 until 1868.

Mill's basic life employment, then, was the work of empire, and this necessarily brought to his attention the current views on the status and qualities of other societies and cultures. Company policy on India was, of course, initially dominated by the concern to make a profit, but the economic motive had to be supplemented by a wider political and social policy. One 'orientalist' or Romantic strand of opinion in British India, associated with the scholar and Bengal judge Sir William Jones, Sir Thomas Munro, Sir John Malcolm, Charles Metcalfe and Mountstuart Elphinstone, appreciated Indian culture on its own terms and resented the attempts at anglicization. Similarly, in France, it was 'Victor Hugo who, along with many French Romantics such as Lammenais, de Maistre, and Lamartine, had a profound respect for the ancient religions of India'.[18] This tendency lost out to those who saw their own country as a model for supposedly more backward peoples to imitate. Thus Lord Cornwallis, Governor-General from 1786 to 1793, had established in Bengal the *zamindari* system, intended to produce a landholding class on the British model. While British aristocrats thought India needed an aristocracy, middle-class critics, James Mill included, thought it needed a middle class. After social structure came religion. Charles Grant, who was on the Court of Directors of the company from 1794 to 1823, was foremost among those concerned to introduce Christianity to the sub-continent.

These various policies, as much disputed concerning India as they were in their application at home, had in common the assumption that India could not be left as it was. For those who now used civilization in the plural, traditional Indian society would be categorized as a civilization, different from that of the

West, but still civilized, and so to be respected in terms of its stable authority structures, systems of law and administration, art, culture and commerce; yet this tendency, so in tune with the mentality of early-nineteenth-century Romanticism, had little appeal to those with actual power. Much more influential where it mattered were the advocates of political economy, Christianity, utilitarianism, rational bureaucracy, and of the supposed glories of the British Constitution. Much divided them and they argued their differences with spirit, persistence and conviction; but they all shared the view that India was an archaic survival with irrational laws and immoral, disgusting habits, and that it urgently needed the reforms that a superior civilization could bring to it. How, then, did James Mill evaluate the Indian society that he was employed to administer? One of his earliest judgements, eight years before the publication of his celebrated *History*, set the tone, for Mill senior denied India the representative institutions he was advocating at home: 'The stage of civilization, and the moral and political situation in which the people of India are placed, render the establishment of legislative assemblies impracticable. A simple form of arbitrary government tempered by European honour and European intelligence, is the only form which is now fit for Hindustan.'[19] Almost sixty years later, in *On Liberty*, his son was to forward a strikingly identical policy 'in dealing with barbarians'.[20] Otherwise it is noteworthy both that James Mill designated his standard of higher civilization not as 'English' or 'British' but as 'European'; and also that the final clause possibly intimates a ladder of development according to which preferable forms of rule might eventually be appropriate.

Utilitarianism is a doctrine with more than a few ambiguities. Its most democratic aspect is the Benthamite notion that all individuals are the judges of their own happiness. No supposedly higher authority can tell people what aims and objects they ought to pursue. The pursuit of ends requires appropriate means, however, and in this the mass of the people would appear to be at a disadvantage. Utilitarianism placed a premium on rational thought. In principle the supposed benefits of any course of action were to be determined by precise calculation. Rationality, then, was the means to social progress and was attainable only by the educated. To a marked extent the utilitarians saw the course of history as a long passage from superstition to rationality. It was in this spirit that Bentham had viewed religion as the ideological arm of state oppression.

For James Mill it was fundamental that 'superstition necessarily gives way, as civilization advances'.[21] In India this had not happened. The society was characterized 'by a system of priestcraft, built upon the most enormous and tormenting superstition that ever harassed and degraded any portion of mankind, their minds were enchained more intolerably than their bodies; in short that, despotism and priestcraft taken together, the Hindus, in mind and body, were the most enslaved portion of the human race'.[22] Thus whatever its other attributes in terms of industry, art and culture, India bore the prime hallmark of a barbarous people. Laws they certainly had, but that was scarcely to their credit, for they enforced 'the cruel and pernicious distinction of castes' and were 'such as could not originate in any other than one of the weakest conditions of the human intellect'.[23] James Mill rejected the notion of an ancient Hindu civilization that had been destroyed by the Mohammedans. India was not merely low on the scale of civilization; it was, in some respects, the lowest of all. He believed that 'the vices of such a system were there carried to a more destructive height *than among any other people*'.[24]

For James Mill the first sign of rising from the bottom rung of development was that a people were able to secure their territory against outsiders. So 'one of the first applications of knowledge is, to improve the military art'. This the Hindus had not done. Neither the necessary understanding nor the discipline was available. One might suppose that a country without military prowess or virtues had lacked the need to develop them. In India, however, peace and tranquillity had been much less common than 'rebellions, massacres, and barbarous conquests'.[25]

We are here still in an age when, in the words of Fania Oz-Salzberger, war 'could imaginably pass for a good thing'[26] and for James Mill militarism had its virtues; not merely through its association with organization and discipline, but also by its encouragement of character, manliness and courage. James Mill never went to India and didn't consider a visit necessary for his research. In terms of his own description one can easily believe that he never wanted to go. Yet in spite of keeping his distance, not a shadow of doubt threatened his self-confident assertions on the character of the people. He noted their 'slavish and dastardly spirit' and how beneath an attractive yet deceptive appearance there 'lies a general disposition to deceit and perfidy'.[27] These weaknesses of Hindu culture had left the people passive, profligate, oppressed, disorganized and vulnerable to foreign invasion.[28]

The Moguls had preceded the French and British in invading India. Their main period of dominance had been from 1527 to 1707. From James Mill's standpoint the very fact of their military success placed them a step above the Hindus on the ladder of civilization. The step seems to have been a rather small one, however, for when Mill got to the issue of moral character, he declared that the Hindu 'ranks very low; and the Mohammedan is little, if at all, above him. The same insincerity, mendacity, and perfidy; the same indifference to the feelings of others; the same prostitution and venality, are conspicuous in both.'[29]

Although we have gained the impression that the Hindus were about as low as a people could get, we also learn that much of the Middle and Far East were similarly placed. James Mill described the Hindus as 'in a state of civilization very nearly the same with that of the Chinese, the Persians, and the Arabians'.[30] In Chapter 6 we shall discuss John Stuart Mill's use of China as the prime example of a civilization that has stagnated, so any discussion of China by his father is of particular interest.

For James Mill the Chinese had an advantage only in 'respect to government and laws'. This seems to have been relatively inconsequential, for otherwise both India and China were placed on the same level. In the arts and sciences Mill thought there was 'a near approximation to the same point of advancement', or rather non-advancement. The same was true in terms of morality and character:

> Both nations are to nearly an equal degree tainted with the vices of insincerity; dissembling, treacherous, mendacious, to an excess which surpasses even the usual measure of uncultivated society. Both are disposed to excessive exaggeration with regard to every thing relating to themselves. Both are cowardly and unfeeling. Both are in the highest degree conceited of themselves, and full of affected contempt for others. Both are in the physical sense, disgustingly unclean in their persons and houses.[31]

In terms of John Stuart Mill's theory of Chinese stagnation it is significant that his father employed this notion in respect of India. This may well have been the son's first acquaintance with the idea, given the age at which he proofread his father's *History*. James Mill believed that Hindu culture had 'been stationary for many ages' so that 'in beholding the Hindus of the present day, we are beholding the Hindus of many ages past; and are carried back, as it were, into the deepest recesses of antiquity'.[32] Clearly here we have not only the notion of a civilization ground to a halt but also the intimation of a general pattern of development; two ideas which were significant components of the son's social analysis.

To James Mill the people of Hindustan appeared inferior in civilization to feudal Europe in religion, philosophy, agriculture and 'in the institutions of government and the laws'. Although the Hindus, 'that effeminate people', were more gentle than 'our ancestors', the latter excelled in manliness and courage. 'In fine,' James Mill decided, 'it cannot be doubted that, upon the whole, the gothic nations, as soon as they become a settled people, exhibit the marks of a superior character and civilization to those of the Hindus.'[33]

Comparative advantage, however, did not imply that England provided the standard to which other countries or cultures should aspire. The utilitarians were also critics of the British political system and believed that poor principles of government at home were replicated abroad. Bentham, for example, believed that 'the English law is a great part of it of such a nature, as to be bad every where'.[34] It was, then, not only in India that cobwebbed and archaic remnants required the cold gleam of rational investigation. James Mill pointed out that Napoleon had been the first European sovereign to codify the laws of his country. In England, by contrast, the common law remained 'in the unwritten, that is, the oral, and traditionary [sic], or barbarous State'.[35] James Mill, though sometimes critical of the East India Company, at least thought that the British ruled India better than the Indians ruled themselves. It cannot have harmed his future employment prospects to have declared:

> in the highly important point of servants or subordinate agents of government, there is nothing in the world to be compared with the East India Company, whose servants as a body, have not only exhibited a portion of talent which forms a contrast with that of the ill-chosen instruments of other governments, but have … maintained a virtue which, under the temptations of their situation is worthy of the highest applause.[36]

It is small wonder, then, that Mill's *History* provided 'a standard work for officials of the East India Company, and eventually became a text-book for candidates for the Indian Civil Service'.[37] Such was its prestige that, in 1859, over forty years after its publication, John Bright made the following point to the House of Commons: 'the Governor-General of India goes out knowing little or nothing of India. I know exactly what he does when he is appointed. He shuts himself up to study the first volumes of Mr. Mill's *History of India*'. Bright, however, was no friend of the East India Company. He then said that the new appointee 'reads through this laborious work without nearly so much effect in making him a good Governor-General as a man might ignorantly suppose'.[38] John Stuart Mill later conceded that he was able to 'perceive deficiencies', which he did not specify, but still thought it 'one of the most instructive histories ever written, and one of the books from which most benefit may be derived by a mind in the course of making up its opinions'.[39] Among the opinions he derived from it was a lesson on how non-Western peoples were to be regarded.

J. S. MILL ON INDIA

For a long time Mill's writings and his employment were regarded as distinct. The former was of interest; the latter was not. The one was in the public domain; the other behind closed doors and so generally out of view. Whereas James Mill had written extensively on India and then later worked for the East India Company, the son worked for the company but did not write a book on India. Lynn Zastoupil has drawn attention to 'Mill's near silence about India in his published works'.[40] Certainly Mill's restraint here was noteworthy given the extraordinary intellectual range over which he provided expert comment. Perhaps he felt the imperative of Civil Service anonymity (and it is from the East India Company that the term 'civil servant' derives); that a servant of the company, whatever his private views, should not be publicly associated with any one policy lest he eventually be compelled to implement its opposite. His work was obviously political, however, for it involved the government of parts of India.

One of the attractions of John Stuart Mill's intellectual work is that he was never narrowly and exclusively theoretical. He referred to his *Principles of Political Economy* as 'not a book merely of abstract science, but also of application'.[41] His concern was always to achieve social progress and so even his philosophical enquiries are related to practical concerns. 'Applications' is the final chapter heading of what is now his best-known work, *On Liberty*. It is, characteristically, the most neglected part of the book, for Mill studies have been dominated by those more concerned with his philosophical contributions. In accord with this, for long Mill's employment, which dealt with the practical issue of drafting policy for various Indian states, did not attract much academic attention. Lynn Zastoupil's *John Stuart Mill and India* has overcome this neglect and demonstrated the interplay between Mill's official work at the India Office and the general development of his ideas.

From the praise he bestowed on his father's history of India one might assume that Mill followed in his footsteps. The reality is less straightforward. Although the son had been taught what to think, he had also been taught *how* to think, and in time the latter came into conflict with the former. The intellectual cramming and narrow rationalist focus of his early education soon took its toll. At the age of twenty Mill had a mental breakdown from which he gradually emerged through acquaintance with Coleridge and the Romantics, who reached parts that austere Benthamism was barely willing to acknowledge. Mill, then, never rejected the utilitarianism with which he had been spoon-fed, though his supposed defence of it in 1861, twenty-five years after his father's death, on some accounts altered it almost beyond recognition.[42] Similarly, while praising his father's researches and policy on India, the son actually went his own way.

It was the father who introduced John Stuart Mill to the India Office, making him initially his unpaid assistant at work as he already was at home. Whereas at home paternal views reigned unchallenged, however, at work James Mill's contempt for Indian culture was modified by a more open-minded understanding. It is, one hopes, true to say that John Stuart shared the radical ends his father pursued, but was more cautious in terms of the means required. His particular blend, then, was of radical aims to be achieved by conservative means. The notion of a hierarchy of cultures was maintained, as was the aim of facilitating progress in a backward society otherwise apparently unable to advance. British domination had in fact been made possible by the inability of the indigenous peoples to combine. In his essay on 'Civilization' Mill noted that 'none but civilized nations have ever been capable of forming an alliance. The native states of India have been conquered by the English one by one.'[43] The clear implication is that Mill did

39

not consider India civilized. Zastoupil suggests that Mill downgraded India for its lack of 'advanced rationality, individual discipline, and social habits of obedience',[44] yet somehow it had still managed to establish towns, commerce, manufacture, agriculture, law and administration. In spite of having these normal criteria of advancement India was still not regarded by Mill even as an ancient civilization that had come to a standstill. It was rather semi-barbarian and so remained at a very early stage of development. On this basis Mill described the Hindus as 'that curious people, who reproduce in so many respects the mental characteristics of the infancy of the human race'.[45]

Under the ideological influence of such British Indian administrators as Munro, Elphinstone and Sir John Malcolm, however, Mill moved nearer to the Burkean view that change had to be organic and gradual, working with and through the institutions and customs that already existed. Lynn Zastoupil has noted that 'imperialism brought Mill into direct contact with some of Burke's ideas and traditional Whig doctrines'.[46]

Edmund Burke, now best known for his attack on the French Revolution, had for most of the 1780s been preoccupied with the attempt to reform the British administration in India. In stark contrast to James Mill a few decades later, Burke encouraged respect for the Indian social structure, religion and political organizations. Such regard, however, had not been forthcoming from the East India Company. In Burke's view they had broken every treaty they had made and 'utterly ruined' every prince or state who had trusted them. Burke's 1783 speech on the East India Company appears, with hindsight, like a dress-rehearsal for his later defence of the French old regime. In both cases it seemed that a settled traditional order had been plundered by rapacious, unprincipled adventurers.

We find a rather Burkean echo in *The Principles of Political Economy* when Mill charged the British in India with having 'grossly misunderstood the usages and rights which it found existing. Its mistakes arose from the inability of ordinary minds to imagine a state of social relations fundamentally different from those with which they are practically familiar.'[47] Mill, then, came to accept 'how very much of the really wonderful acquiescence of mankind in any government which they find established, is the effect of mere habit and imagination' and that this 'cannot transfer itself easily to new institutions, even though in themselves preferable'.[48] He did not go as far as the pure orientalists, who saw a fundamental and often deep value in traditional ways. What Mill acquired instead was an administrative realism concerning the deeply rooted facts of Indian life. These could not be wished away, nor swept out without producing immensely counter-productive resistance. India provided no *tabula rasa*. Not even James Mill could treat India as he had done his son: as empty terrain on which a utilitarian edifice could be constructed. It was Rousseau who conceded that ideal laws could be given only to a people who had not previously been corrupted. The Mills would not have called India an ancient civilization; but certainly it had a traditional culture, whose deeply embedded practices had already endured and survived earlier invasions. The British were immensely outnumbered in India. It has been estimated that in the nineteenth century they were ruling about a hundred million people, very many more than the population of their home country. It was prudential realism to insist that they could govern only through the co-operation and, at least, partial consent and tolerance, of the Indian people themselves. Zastoupil notes that, in a dispatch of 1828, Mill called for 'the extensive use of Indians, even at the highest levels, in any British administration of Awadh'.[49] This was an upward modification of the more usual policy by which a stratum of Indians was given employment in the lower levels of both the administration and the army, thereby providing them with a vested interest in the forms of British rule. Years later independent India's first Prime Minister noted that 'British rule thus consolidated itself by creating new classes and vested interests who were tied up with that rule and whose privileges depended on its continuance.'[50]

Though he defended the role of the East India Company and, indeed, in its last days was its foremost advocate, Mill was never an unequivocal supporter of its various policies; nor could he, or anyone else, have been, given the various shifts of emphasis that had occurred. If not an actual part of the British state, then the company had at least a close affinity with it, certainly in terms of its assumptions and class of personnel. As a critic of the dominant and traditional policies of the British state at home, Mill could hardly avoid opposing similar elements that existed in the East India Company. In an 1828 dispatch Mill feared that the British were using their troops to bolster traditional despotism. Thus the 'shortsightedness and rapacity of a semi-barbarous Government is armed with the military strength of a civilized one'.[51] Just as Mill opposed the British Government for tolerating a negligent and corrupt aristocracy in Ireland, so he condemned the *zamindari* system introduced into Bengal: 'England being accustomed to great estates and great landlords, the English rulers took it for granted that India must possess the like.' The landlordism that had been so disastrous in the one instance, however, had now 'proved a total failure' in the other. 'The new landed aristocracy' of Bengal 'disappointed every expectation built upon them. They did nothing for the improvement of their estates, but everything for their own ruin.'[52]

In Bengal, as in Ireland, Mill recommended creating a class of peasant proprietors who, freed from the clutches of feudalistic dues or burdensome rents, would have an interest in the fruitful development of their own land. Mill's home and foreign policy were just as equally co-ordinated on the matter of religion as they were on peasant proprietorship and just as in England he opposed the provision of education by religious organizations, so in India he disliked the attempts of the Clapham Sect, led by William Wilberforce and Charles Grant, to use Christianity to bind the Indians to British rule.

These affinities of policy, however, were not matched by a proposal for similar governmental forms; for what was appropriate for the one was not so for the other. Great Britain was civilized and hence fit for self-government; India was, at best, seen as 'semi-barbarous', and so most suited to being a dependency. In *Representative Government* Mill remarked that it 'has been the destiny of the government of the East India Company, to suggest the true theory of the government of a semi-barbarous dependency by a civilized country'.[53] It is, then, to Mill's justification of imperialism that we must now turn.

THE JUSTIFICATION OF IMPERIALISM

The utilitarian discussion of India preceded both Mills. Long before either of them was in the India Office, Jeremy Bentham had poured scorn on the whole enterprise. In an essay published in 1782 Bentham noted the common view that the 'passion of avarice has implanted among the inhabitants of English race in Bengal, two evil propensities; a propensity to practice [*sic*] extortion, to the prejudice of the subjected Asiatics; and a propensity to practice peculation, to the prejudice of the public revenue'. How, he then asked, must this have looked to the 'poor Hindus'? It must surely have seemed like a 'deliberate plan for forcing' them 'without reserve, into the hands of the European professional blood-suckers, carrying on the traffic of injustice under the cloak of law'.[54]

In 1793 Bentham sent Talleyrand a pamphlet entitled 'Emancipate Your Colonies!'.[55] It was in some ways a rather strange piece. Bentham's advice to the French was argued on the basis of colonialism being in contradiction with their declared revolutionary principles. He did not mention that those principles, based on theories of abstract rights, were not his own. In that sense the pamphlet was rather opportunistic. He hoped that once the French had freed their colonies, the British would then follow their example. Bentham, says Halévy, 'up to the end of his life stood as an adversary of the colonial system'.[56] Here, however, we must distinguish between two different kinds of colonial venture. What, on the whole, Bentham opposed was the imposition of European rule on non-European peoples. The British had exported to India the whole panoply of aristocratic privilege and corruption down to the fictions, delays and absurdities of their common-law courts. 'And who would think it? This mass of absurdity is the work of modern refinement, not of ancient barbarism.'[57]

The colonialism that Bentham came to approve was that of voluntary British settlement overseas as a means of dealing with the 'surplus population'. Here a British overseas colony is ruling itself rather than imposing external rule on a foreign people. The difference between the two types is obviously obfuscated by them sharing a common term. In 1831, the last full year of his long life, Bentham was converted to Edward Wakefield's plans for systematic emigration and drew up a charter for a colony in south Australia. He gave it the splendidly utilitarian name of Felicitania. When two years later the South Australian Association was formed, its forty-two members included a number of Bentham's followers, among them John Stuart Mill. The actual colony was founded in 1836 and so, according to Halévy, who obviously enjoyed the irony, 'it happened that the Benthamites were the founders of the English Australasian colonies'.[58]

Colonies of settlement, in so far as there are no indigenous people in the area, or – a dubious proposition – that such people are not affected, pose no great difficulties from a utilitarian perspective. Such colonies could be defended on the basis of the greatest good, both for those who remained in Britain and for those who formed the settlement. The situation of indigenous peoples who have foreign rule imposed on them was, of course, quite different.

We should initially note that the establishment of government at all is problematic for, in one sense at least, the logic of utilitarianism points in an anarchist direction. In a number of places Bentham asserted that individuals are themselves the best judges of what tends to their own happiness.[59] In that case we might ask why there should be law at all, for the main purpose of law is to stop people doing what they otherwise would. Bentham's answer is that mankind is happier with law than it would be without it. If every person were the rational agent that Bentham assumed, however, then incurring punishment by breaking the law would not occur, though law-breaking might occur among those who knew how to avoid being caught! Indeed, the very making of law, for the purpose of guidance towards the general happiness, assumes there are people who need such guidance; who are therefore unable otherwise to perceive either their own or the general happiness. Bentham did mention that infancy and insanity were grounds for exclusion, and in *The Principles of Morals and Legislation* both asserted and then denied that women were incapable of making rational, utilitarian calculations.[60] On this logic law had to exist because of them. From this basis, there could be no utilitarian justification for colonial rule over other peoples, unless, as was commonly the case, they were collectively regarded as juvenile, belonging to cultures still in the infancy of civilized development, and that there were others in authority over them who were reliably able to perceive their interests for them.

But yet, in spite of the theory, 'Colonisation is a fact beyond which their logic capitulated … Bentham had always dreamed of making laws for India.'[61] Already in 1782 Bentham imagined replacing the narrow and archaic bounds of current colonial rule with governors able to ascertain the greatest happiness of the greatest number. Such legislators 'having freed themselves from the shackles of authority, have learnt to soar above the mists of prejudice, know as well how to make laws for one country as for another: all they need is to be possessed fully of the facts'.[62] Once James Mill was established in the East India Company, Bentham hoped that his own ideas might attain dominance. 'I shall be the dead legislative of British India,' he decided. 'Twenty years after I am dead, I shall be a despot.'[63] For James Mill, too, in spite of his *History of British India*, the practice of imperialism posed problems for his philosophical system. Though the Indian people were regarded as backward and in need of development, it is hard to see how even Benthamite rulers could be trusted to serve a society that had not elected them. In 1820, just one year after his appointment to the British East India Company, James Mill's 'Essay on Government' was published. Here we learn that good government has to be representative and that the representative body 'must have an identity of interest with the community; otherwise it will make a mischievous use of its power'. This proposition was evidently one 'about which it is unlikely that there will be any dispute'.[64] Surely all colonialism is thereby implicitly condemned; not that Mill here drew this conclusion. Even were we to concede that a people stand in need of advancement, we still find in James Mill no means by which unelected rulers can avoid degenerating into a 'sinister interest'. It was John Bright who applied this point to India, noting that under the rule of the British East India Company 'there is no sort of tie between the governors and the governed'.[65]

Another side of utilitarianism, however, allows an answer which makes it compatible with imperialism. In utilitarianism the end is the greatest happiness rather than the greatest participation. Alan Ryan has made the point that for James Mill, 'if we were able to find a government which, for reasons other than the restraints imposed by elections, pursued the general interest, it would be as good as a democratic government. The implications for the British in India hardly need to be spelled out.'[66] Consequentialism, then, provides a justification for imperialism. The people are having good done for them. We could further mention that the implications for the mass of the British in Britain also hardly need to be spelled out. Democracy, then, like any other form of government, is not seen as an end in itself; it is merely a means. If the greatest good of the greatest number is more likely to be achieved in some other way, as it certainly was for believers in elite expertise, then that other way would be preferable. Ryan had earlier pointed out that 'One of the ways in which Bentham and James Mill stood outside the mainstream of liberalism is that they both believed that so long as government operates for the benefit of the governed, their actual participation in their own government is immaterial.'[67] The utilitarians were thus caught in a bind. They believed that an educated administrative elite knows what is best, but also that if unchecked it is liable to become corrupt. The only check is that of the people, but if their level is such that they do not qualify for participation then they simultaneously are disqualified from providing a check. An irrational people are not qualified to check their rulers, and so their rulers are not safeguarded against degenerating into a partial interest.

In 1820 James Mill had also published a short article on colonization in the *Encyclopaedia Britannica*. His friend and biographer Alexander Bain was unimpressed. There was a weary note to his finding that 'Bentham had likewise gone over the ground and come to much the same conclusions'.[68] There is, however, a rather piquant difference between the anti-colonialism of Bentham and that of James Mill, for the latter was already an employee of the East India Company when he wrote his article. This was anything but obvious, for James Mill presented the issue in a context that had no relevance to India, that of how Britain was to dispose of its 'surplus' population. Otherwise he took colonialism to be largely a matter of economics. His one comment on India was that 'instead of yielding a tribute to England' it had 'never yielded enough for the expence [*sic*] of its own government ... it has cost this country enormous sums'. This was due to no particular lapse by his employers but was rather the normal colonial condition. 'The policy of holding a colony for the benefit of its trade, is, therefore, a bad policy.'[69]

What then, one is bound to ask, is colonialism for, at least outside of the more temperate regions to which the 'surplus' poor could emigrate? James Mill's answer was pure Paine and Cobbett. The colonies provided powerful and prestigious places for the surplus rich. 'There are governorships and judge-ships, and a long train of *et ceteras*' and as a grand source of wars the colonies helped extend the state apparatus for the benefit of the few. There was nothing on the justification of one people ruling another, a particularly important issue, it would seem, in the light of James Mill's conviction that 'at the distance of a colony' the restraints on bad government 'operate with diminished force'.[70]

A decade later his son was also pondering the problems of bad government. Here, however, it was less the bad government of the colonizer than of a backward society. Already in his fourth 'Spirit of the Age' article John Stuart Mill declared that one characteristic of such societies was an inability to provide good government.[71] An only slightly more optimistic version occurred years later in a famous passage from *On Liberty*, where Mill implied that very exceptional individuals could act as agents of improvement. It was clearly not easy for a backward society to advance. 'The early difficulties in the way of spontaneous progress are so great, that there is seldom any choice of means for overcoming them.' Therefore a 'ruler full of the spirit of improvement is warranted in the use of any expedients that will attain an end, perhaps otherwise unattainable'. It was for this reason that

> Despotism is a legitimate mode of government in dealing with barbarians, provided that the end be their improvement, and the means justified by actually effecting that end. Liberty, as a principle, has no application to any state of things anterior to the time when mankind have become capable of

45

being improved by free and equal discussion. Until then, there is nothing for them but implicit obedience to an Akbar or a Charlemagne, if they are so fortunate to find one.[72]

What is implicit but clear here is that liberty is not a human right. Mill found it axiomatic that 'we may leave out of consideration those backward states of society in which the race itself may be considered as in its nonage'.[73] It was in such a category that he had always placed India.

So the country whose government was the sole concern of Mill's employment did not come within the scope of his most famous principle. The Indian people were not yet fit recipients of liberty, which would become their due only at a later stage of development. In June 1852, Mill had informed a House of Lords committee that 'the public of India afford no assistance in their government. They are not ripe for doing so by means of representative government.'[74] Only occasionally had reform come from within to a barbarian people. Finding an Akbar or a Charlemagne is 'fortunate' not because it dispenses with despotism, but because it uses it to achieve some primary steps of development. Charlemagne (742–814) was a remarkable military leader who had consolidated an empire that stretched across Europe from the Ebro to the Elbe. Mill's approval is more likely to have been won for his knowledge of Latin and Greek and his encouragement of education, agriculture, arts, commerce and manufacture. Akbar (1542–1605) had also been successful militarily, bringing most of northern India under Mogul control, but as with Charlemagne, he had considerable cultural achievements to his credit. He had encouraged literature and was sufficiently tolerant of other religions to have requested that missionaries from Goa give him an account of Christianity. He had also promoted commerce by constructing roads, introducing a uniform system of weights and measures, organizing an efficient police system and making reforms in taxation.

The point about indigenous benevolent despotism was reiterated a few years after *On Liberty* in *Considerations on Representative Government*. Mill was now a bit more explicit: 'In a country not under the domination of foreigners, the only cause adequate to producing similar benefits is the rare accident of a monarch of extraordinary genius.'[75] Here again two examples were given. Charlemagne was acclaimed as before, but Akbar was replaced by Peter the Great. Here Mill followed Bentham, who had instanced Peter's civilizing influence in *The Theory of Legislation*[76] and thought these were rare examples of the reforms remaining as a permanent legacy. Mill's analysis is controversial, for Charlemagene's empire fell to pieces under his successors whereas, according to Nehru, Akbar's system was accepted by his son and grandson, before being partially undone by their successor, Aurungzeb.[77]

A people not fit for liberty is clearly not fit for representative government and hardly even for self-government. In his *Autobiography* Mill recalled his acceptance of the Saint-Simonian view that institutions relate to the level of development of the society, so that different stages require different political institutions. He noted how he 'ceased to consider representative democracy as an absolute principle, and regarded it as a question of time, place, and circumstance' which 'ought to be decided mainly by the consideration, what great improvement in life and culture stands *next in order* for the people concerned, as the condition of their further progress'.[78] This is the view that we also find in *Representative Government*, a principle of apparently recent acceptance, for in what Mill called 'the last age' it had, absurdly in his view, been 'customary to claim representative democracy for England or France by arguments which would equally have proved it the only fit form of government for Bedouins or Malays'.[79]

It was precisely because different institutions fitted different stages of development that Mill felt able to accept the Roman Catholic Church as having been a positive force in medieval Europe. Similarly, for his own time, Mill believed that government by a developed people could be an advantage for a backward society. Given his father's perspective, one can understand how he was led to assume that some peoples were not fitted for self-government and so in need of an advanced, enlightened elite to rule over them. James Mill had 'strenuously resisted any suggestion for establishing representative institutions for India'.[80]

Two of Mill's most illuminating writings dealing with the justification of colonialism, the relationship between the colonial and the colonized powers and the criteria which fit some for, and hence exclude others from, self-government, were published at about the same time as *On Liberty*. Even more significantly, these were the years immediately following the 1857 Indian Mutiny and the assumption by the British state of direct rule over India. These works were the short and little-known 'A Few Words on Non-Intervention', published in *Fraser's Magazine* in December 1859, and the more celebrated *Consideration on Representative Government*, which appeared two years later.

In 'A Few Words on Non-Intervention' we find an enlargement of the attitude towards barbarians already familiar from *On Liberty*. For Mill there were never any doubts concerning the division between 'us' and 'them', by which those who declared themselves civilized designated all others as 'barbarian'. Interestingly for an agnostic, Mill accepted 'Christian Europe' as 'members of an equal community of nations' whose conduct towards one another necessarily follows different rules from that towards others. There are, then, two codes of behaviour, for to 'suppose that the same international customs, and the same rule of international morality, can obtain between one civilized nation and another, and between civilized nations and barbarians, is a grave error'. For precisely that reason

Mill declared that the 'criticisms, therefore, which are so often made upon the conduct of the French in Algeria, or of the English in India, proceed, it would seem, mostly on a wrong principle'.[81]

Mill presumed it self-evident into which category each society belonged, civilized or barbarian. The consequence of this is that the society that presumes the lower category of the other simultaneously decides which morality to treat it with! Mill's justification was that relations between nations are conducted according to rules of reciprocity that barbarians cannot understand or implement. 'They cannot be depended on for observing any rules. Their *minds* are not capable of so great an effort.'[82] As in *On Liberty*, the fundamental divide is one of mental development. A people not fit for liberty is neither civilized nor ready for representative government and would be incapable of making good use even of self-government.

This brings us to what seems to be the key point of the essay, the justification of imperial rule. 'Nations which are still barbarian have not got beyond the period during which it is likely to be for their benefit that they should be conquered and held in subjection by foreigners.' Here for once Mill referred to 'barbarous nations', more usually regarded as an oxymoron, for a normal characteristic of barbarian peoples was their inability to achieve national unity. Even if they did: 'Independence and nationality, so essential to the due growth and development of a people further advanced in improvement, are generally impediments to theirs.'[83] So peoples not yet fit for liberty are probably the same as those also not ready for independence and nationality. Furthermore, we now have what seems a blatantly weak rationale. The barbarians have no rights as a nation because they aren't one, or, if they are, then no rights as a nation because, on account of their low developmental level, they shouldn't be one. Therefore, to 'characterize any conduct whatever towards a barbarous people as a violation of the law of nations, only shows that he who so speaks has never considered the subject'. In its context one could plausibly assume that for Mill the law of nations applies only to nations. Ten years earlier, however, Mill had made it plain that he did not believe in such a law.[84]

The obvious point now is to ask by what principle a people who are not a nation is to be protected from abuse. Mill's answer and protective principle here is the unspecified 'universal rules of morality between man and man'.[85] This, then, is the bottom line. Barbarians are defended by 'the universal rules of morality'. The civilized enjoy those rules plus something rather more advanced, although with nearly the same name; that is the 'rule of ordinary international morality'.[86] These imply reciprocity, of which barbarians are not capable. The civilized, then, can make more moral effective claims between their respective nations and so are, in that respect, better protected. How much better is difficult to ascertain without knowing more precisely how much ground lies between these two principles. Certainly those designated as civilized are the appropriate judges of what constitutes proper treatment, and that right is a strength in itself. We see here how difficult it is to find a ground for principles of behaviour when both religion and a belief in natural human rights are rejected. Utilitarian justifications are not explicit here, but Mill's reference to the backward state of barbarian 'minds' does not suggest that they are capable of applying the felicific calculus.

Mill further assumed that barbarians were bound to be aggressive and that a neighbouring civilized country would, sooner or later, have to conquer them. In this way the barbarians become dependent on their civilized conquerors, who therefore 'become morally responsible for all evil it allows them to do. This is the history of the relations of the British Government with the native States of India.' Even were we to accept that the Indians were 'barbarous' it was somewhat disingenuous of Mill to designate them as 'barbarous neighbours'. As neighbours the English had the Welsh and the Scots, seeing as here Mill refers to 'the English in India'.[87] The Indians were far away, effectively much more so than today given the available means of transport and communication. The governments that became 'neighbours' did so only as a *consequence* of English (or British) conquest on the sub-continent, yet Mill is here using the unruly neighbours argument to justify that conquest in the first place.

It would, presumably, be ideal if those merely fit to be colonized were to be ruled by those fit to do so. Each people would then be in a position appropriate to its capacities. Mill, however, was a much greater defender of the principle than of the practice of colonial rule. The practice had too often fallen below the required standard. This lapse had, it seems, to be accepted; it was almost inevitable and certainly had fewer disadvantages than any alternative. Already in antiquity it was clear that the 'Romans were not the most clean-handed of conquerors, yet would it have been better for Gaul and Spain, Numidia and Dacia, never to have formed part of the Roman Empire?'[88] The same point still applied.

All in all, this short essay does not find Mill at his most convincing. Many of the statements are vague and the arguments are weak. At times his tone is unusually tetchy, possibly the cover for a weak argument. After all his years in the India Office one might have expected Mill to have thought through a better justification for the exercise of the rule in which he was employed. The agnostic refers to 'sacred duties',[89] defines civilization as constituting Christian Europe, and defends imperialism as a means of improvement yet admits that often it hasn't been. 'A Few Words on Non-Intervention' can be regarded as a revealing though less than satisfactory first draft of parts of the better-known and more thorough *Considerations on Representative Government*, to which we now turn.

It was in his work on *Representative Government* that Mill most fully discussed the criteria which made a people fit for it. In terms of our present concerns we shall concentrate on Mill's views on the unfitness of India for self-government and on the qualifications the British had for ruling over them.

Mill thought that some dependencies were 'ripe' for representative government because they were 'composed of people of similar civilization to the ruling country'. This was the case for Australia and for 'the British possessions in America', which presumably refers to Canada. 'Others, like India, are still at a great distance from that state.' Mill here also referred to India as an example of a country 'not fit to govern itself'. There can also be little doubt that Mill had India in mind when designating a country 'unfitted for representative government ... by extreme passiveness, and ready submission to tyranny'.[90] In such a country even 'the One and his counsellors, or the Few', that is the elite on whom Mill otherwise usually relied, would not be fit agents of improvement, unless they were 'foreigners, belonging to a superior people or a more advanced state of society'. In this instance, 'subjection to a foreign government of this description, notwithstanding its inevitable evils, is often of the greatest advantage to a people, carrying them rapidly through several stages of progress, and clearing away obstacles to improvement which might have lasted indefinitely if the subject population had been left unassisted to its native tendencies and chances'.[91] We should additionally remind ourselves that *Representative Government* was published just a few years after the Indian Mutiny. From the British perspective it would have seemed risible to suggest Indian independence at that time. Even stricter control was the generally presumed recommendation, and this is what direct British rule was intended to produce.

Liberalism, like all other '-isms', is a contested concept, but it has long been associated with freedom and government based on consent. Here, however, in the writings of a man regarded as one of Britain's foremost liberal thinkers, we find a defence of a despotic form of government imposed by foreign conquerors. Such a '*mode of government*', Mill tells us, '*is as legitimate as any other*'[92] so long as it helps to raise a backward people to a higher level of civilization.

Was this, then, a condition which the British were able to provide? Had the need of one people for improvement coincided with their rule by another people able to supply it? As has already been evident, Mill's answers to these questions were ambivalent. In a diary entry from the 1850s he noted that 'Perhaps the English are the fittest people to rule over barbarous or semi-barbarous nations like those of the East, precisely because they are the stiffest, and most wedded to their own customs, of all civilized people.'[93] In this instance the British narrow-minded imperviousness to foreign cultural influences, which Mill criticized when it excluded the ideas of the French, seemed to serve as an advantage. Mill thought that all previous conquerors, including the Portuguese, had at least partially gone native and been absorbed by the country they had conquered. This too would have happened to the French had they been given the chance. The British, however, had kept their distance, imposing an effective barrier between themselves and the Indians. This account is at least partially confirmed from the other side by Jawaharlal Nehru, who noted how India had absorbed the Moghul conquerors but that, in contrast, the British had kept themselves totally separate.[94]

In *Representative Government* Mill noted that 'Free States, like all others, may possess dependencies, acquired either by conquest or by colonization; and our own is the greatest instance of the kind in modern history.' He also mentioned that 'our rule in India has lasted, and been one of constant, if not very rapid, improvement in prosperity and good administration'. Even so it is still 'always under great difficulties, and very imperfectly, that a country can be governed by foreigners' and 'in the case of India, a politically active people like the English, amidst habitual acquiescence, are every now and then interfering, and almost always in the wrong place'. Among other complaints, Mill thought it wrong to 'force English ideas down the throats of the natives', as was being done with Christianity. It seemed to him that the British, in common with other colonial rulers, failed adequately to protect the weak. In India the 'European settlers ... think the people of the country mere dirt under their feet: it seems to them monstrous that any rights of the natives should stand in the way of their smallest pretensions.'[95] Mill was very aware of the class structure within Indian society and thought that only the more powerful had access to the British authorities. In the years after the Mutiny, as India came under direct British state rule, it seemed increasingly clear that the British were allowing the dominant landed classes more power than ever, and this at the expense of the peasantry. It was the opposite of the policy he had always recommended, in both India and Ireland, as the means to increase agricultural output by giving the peasantry the security and incentive to pursue prosperity.

Most of this should be hardly surprising, for as the Mills were quite critical of how the British had ruled themselves, one might scarcely expect them to be less so of how they ruled others. Their judgement of British rule in India, however, with which they were, of course, professionally involved, remained less adverse than their estimate of British rule at home.

Nevertheless, on balance the British seemed better at ruling others than at ruling themselves. One might suggest that if the record of self-government were held as a test for colonial rule, then the Mills, so critical of home governments, would have had to declare the British disqualified. There is, then, a degree of paradox in their position. For more conservative writers the presumed excellence of British institutions and customs could serve as a qualifying criterion for ruling over others. For the Mills the reverse might seem to apply. Fundamental criticism of home institutions is not the most propitious basis for justifying colonial rule. It seemed that the Mills' policy was for colonial rule to be carried out according to the most advanced and rational ideas; that is British rule, according to utilitarian criteria, and thus purged of the archaisms that hindered reform at home. India too, of course, had its archaisms, perhaps older and more deeply entrenched even than those of Britain, but colonial rule, as a form of benevolent despotism, had the power that was unavailable at home to make rapid strides forward.

In this sense we see how imperialism could be incorporated into both conservative and radical creeds. In both cases there was the presumption of superiority. For the conservatives it was deemed sufficient to bring law and order to peoples unable to achieve it autonomously. For the radicals this was also true, but additionally it seemed progressive to bring 'backward' peoples into the modern world. This was clearly the view Mill held of the British in India and much the same applies to Marx. For Marx traditional Indian village life was 'undignified, stagnant, and vegetative'. 'English interference' had 'dissolved these small semi-barbarian, semi-civilised communities, by blowing up their economical basis, and thus produced the greatest, and to speak the truth, the only *social* revolution ever heard of in Asia'.[96]

We have mentioned that Mill did not apply to backward peoples the liberal principle of government by consent. This was traditionally just one of the means by which liberals sought to control the powers of the state. Liberals, though, were no anarchists; they saw the state as necessary but dangerous. It, therefore, had to be limited and controlled and the recommended devices to this end included a written constitution, separation of powers, federalism, the explicit codification and defence of human rights, and the confinement of the state to 'night-watchman' functions to the exclusion of significant measures of economic control.

Now just as liberty did not apply to a backward people, so neither did other aspects of the liberal package. Mill regarded the peoples of the East as accustomed to despotism. Their low levels of education and individuality left them unable to manage without it. The only option was between tyrannical and benevolent despotism and so Mill pointed out that the 'proper functions of a government are not a fixed thing, but different in different states of society; much *more extensive* in a backward than in an advanced state'.[97] In one sense Mill was a great believer in hierarchy. Some individuals were more cultivated than others and some societies more civilized than others. For some conservative thinkers hierarchy was inevitable, permanent and divinely ordained. Burke, for example, wrote of the 'inviolable oath which holds all physical and all moral natures, each in their appointed place'.[98] In Mill's time the climatic determinism of Montesquieu was still influential. Mill was a contemporary of Gobineau, for whom racial characteristics placed limits on what each individual could attain. For Mill, however, hierarchies were fluid. Individuals could strive to become more cultivated and societies could ascend further up the ladder of civilization. The notion of a civilizing mission is open to obvious objections, but it does at least do colonized peoples the honour of assuming that their advancement is possible. It both designates a gulf between ruling and subject peoples yet concedes or at least intimates that, in the long term, that gulf is bridgeable. In principle, then, the future for both individuals and societies was quite open-ended. No peoples were barred from further development, though some might find it easier to attain than others.

This outlook has an obvious bearing on Mill's attitude to imperialism. The civilizing mission was to bring law, order, good institutions and education to societies without them. In *The Principles of Political Economy* Mill explained that state action was justifiable only if its function was transitional towards enabling people to manage on their own. We shall consider whether he held to the same logic in terms of imperial rule; that its justification was in raising a people to the level at which they were ready for self-government. In a memorandum he wrote in the India Office, Mill recommended that the 'British Government should undertake the management of [Awadh], in the name of the King, *for such a period as* may be found necessary for restoring order, and for establishing an efficient system of administration'.[99] The italicized words indicate that Mill's recommendation was for a temporary period.

In an 1830 dispatch on the problems of Kathiawr, Mill voiced his optimism that the East India Company had been able to rescue its charges from the semi-barbarism in which it had found them. He noted that the old martial culture had significantly declined and that the society was in 'transition to a more advanced stage of improvement'. The practices of 'a semibarbarous age' had not

> been able to maintain themselves against the progress of civilization ... The virtues which it is now in our power, and must be our business to cultivate in the higher classes of India, are not those of a military Chieftain, but of a civilized man ... The same change of circumstances enables us ... to aspire to the even more enviable distinction, of advancing the body of the people in comfort, intelligence, and orderly habits, far beyond what they have reached under even the best Native Governments of India.[100]

What, then, was the destination towards which advancement might lead? If childhood leads to adulthood, and barbarism to civilization, then presumably colonialism eventually results in independence. This seems to be the logic of Mill's position and it is a strong presumption in recent commentaries. T. R. Metcalf, for example, believes that Mill thought 'good government and education could so transform India's peoples that in the end their claim to freedom would be irresistible'. He thinks that John Stuart Mill was not 'alone in looking forward *without hesitation* to the eventual end of British rule'.[101] We find a similar view in William Stafford's recent book. Mill, he tells us, 'thought that an imperial power should take steps to improve its subjects, and as they improved they should participate in their own government; eventually they would become self-governing, perhaps as dependencies, as had happened to Canada'.[102] This seems to be the normal interpretation.

Alan Ryan believes that 'Mill was not in the usual sense an imperialist', though the plausibility of this judgement would depend on what the 'usual sense' is taken to be. A. P. Thornton, among others, has shown that many stripes of imperialist existed, from which we can conclude that if Mill was not 'usual', neither was he that unusual in respect of his broad doctrines of imperial rule.[103] He was at least enough of an imperialist to devote thirty-five years of his professional life to serving British rule in India. Ryan continues, however: Mill 'had no particular enthusiasm for imperial projects, and thought that once the British had given the Indian subcontinent the tools of self-government, their next task was to go home and leave the Indians to work out their own destiny'.[104]

Ryan had earlier made the same point:

> For James Mill, who saw in government few questions other than those of cheapness, orderliness and effectiveness, the despotism of Britain over Asia was no temporary staging post on the way to some other form of association. But for J. S. Mill, the stage of despotic government can only be justified if it really is a stage on the way to self-rule and independence.[105]

As evidence Ryan footnotes the famous passage in *On Liberty* about 'implicit obedience to an Akbar or a Charlemagne', which continues as follows:

> But as soon as mankind have attained the capacity of being guided to their own improvement by conviction or persuasion (a period long since reached in all nations with whom we need here concern ourselves), compulsion, either in the direct form or in that of pains and penalties for non-compliance, is no longer admissible as a means to their own good, and justifiable only for the security of others.[106]

Here Mill wrote about the conditions which would render the continuation of despotism unjustifiable; the issue is put in negative terms, those of despotism not continuing, rather than explicitly facing up to the issue of popular rule. It is noteworthy that barbarian people are offered only the positive hopes of the benevolent despotism of an Akbar or a Charlemagne. It is perhaps significant that in this passage Mill did not include the benefits of 'implicit obedience' to the East India Company. Thus the end of despotism that he was envisaging was more likely to have been the removal of Akbar and Charlemagne, of indigenous despots, rather than the end of colonial rule. If that really were his wish and prognosis he certainly could have learnt something from Bentham and said so more directly.

Ryan's case, then, is in need of more explicit evidence. This he provided a few pages later, drawing on Mill's answers to a parliamentary select committee in 1852–53. Ryan believes that Mill here 'put forward his view that the elevation of the native population to self-rule was part of the object of the Company's government: "in proportion as the natives become trustworthy and qualified for high office, it seems to me not only allowable, but a duty to appoint them to it".' Mill was then asked: 'Do you think that in those circumstances, the dependence of India on this country could be maintained?' He replied: 'I think it might, by judicious management, be made to continue till the time arises when the natives shall be qualified to carry on the same system of Government without our assistance.'[107]

It is not clear that this passage supports Ryan's claim that Indian self-rule was actually the *'object* of the Company's government', which sounds a bit too purposive. One might equally read the passage to imply that the company should continue its rule as long as possible but that such rule becomes unjustifiable once the Indians themselves are qualified to 'carry on *the same system of Government* without our assistance'. The italicized words indicate that, even if self-rule were conceded, Mill was still locked into the imperialist notion of a civilizing mission. Self-government here does not seem to mean independence for a people free to govern itself according to its own beliefs. Instead the Indians were to continue in the way they had been taught by their colonial masters.

Nevertheless, these accounts certainly follow the *logic* of Mill's position; that imperial rule served to elevate a backward people through education and sound administration, and also that a cultivated, civilized people are ripe for self-government. We should note, however, that *contra* Metcalf, Stafford and Ryan, Mill was far from explicit in pushing this logic to its full conclusion. *Representative Government* was a work of Mill's mature period, written after he had retired from the East India Company, and so free from any restraints on the expression of his opinions. In it we find the following:

> But though Great Britain could do perfectly well without her colonies, and though on every principle of morality and justice she ought to consent to their separation, should the time come when, after full trial of the best form of union, they deliberately desire to be dissevered; there are strong reasons for maintaining the present slight bond of connexion, so long as not disagreeable to the feelings of either party.[108]

In a work that devoted many pages to British and other imperialisms this long and rather ungainly sentence was the nearest Mill came to considering colonial independence. It is not exactly an unequivocal recommendation. Note that the issue of morality and justice is related only to a time, which might not even come, when 'full trial of the best form of union' has taken place. What we find here is considerably less than the belief, let alone the recommendation, of imperial rule leading naturally to independence. Rather, independence is merely and vaguely alluded to as a possibility. Our case here is strengthened by the fact that this passage is from a section dealing *only* with Britain's 'colonies of European race', that is 'people of similar civilisation to the ruling country, capable of, and ripe for, representative government'.[109] If not even they qualify for full independence we shall not be surprised to find that in the section on those not fit for representative government, the question of future independence does not even arise.

The above analysis is more than confirmed by Mill's writings on British government of Ireland. In 1846 he wrote that 'We have had the Irish all to ourselves, for five hundred years ... They have been as completely delivered into our hands as children into those of their parents and instructors.' The result was 'the most unqualified instance of signal failure which the practical genius of the English people has exhibited'.[110] This was not exactly an advertisement for British rule, yet Mill's consistent view was that British rule should continue, but on an improved basis. In an 1834 newspaper article he concluded that: 'We have been far too guilty in our treatment of Ireland, to be entitled to shake her off, and let her alone abide the consequences of our misconduct. We are bound not to renounce the government of Ireland, but to govern her well.'[111] A similar view can be found in Mill's 1868 essay on 'England and Ireland'.[112]

Mill's writings on the colonial relationship are not the finest examples of his logical powers. There is a certain diffidence in pushing through the implications of his argument. This is somewhat uncharacteristic of the man who wrote so unequivocally and courageously in:

1. Condemning centuries of British misrule in Ireland and putting the case of the Irish poor at the time of the great famine.[113]
2. Publicly supporting the 1848 revolution in France at a time when the established order in Britain was still fearful of the example it set.[114]
3. Giving a very fair hearing to the case for socialism in his *Principles of Political Economy.*[115]
4. Condemning the massacre by Governor Eyre in Jamaica in spite of opposition from the mass of public opinion in Britain.[116]
5. ... and the cause that subjected him to the greatest ridicule, that of combating *The Subjection of Women.*[117]

Mill followed his father in writing on education, economics and utilitarianism, yet where we have James Mill's six long volumes on the *History of British India* the son produced little more than scattered remarks on the subject. As U. S. Mehta has recently pointed out – and others less recently – liberalism and empire made a strange combination.[118] Rights, freedom, democracy, autonomy, representative government and independence all fail at the hurdle of ripeness. The liberal rights were, then, not universal. One had to qualify for them by being sufficiently mature, and in Mill's view most of the world wasn't.

This listing of liberal components indicates that liberalism has a *set* of values. We can agree with Isaiah Berlin that the idea of a liberal utopia is incoherent because the values are incommensurate.[119] We here see how Mill's developmentalism trumps other values; most strikingly, in Mill's famous confession in the introductory chapter of *On Liberty*, it trumps liberty, which is not for everyone, but only for those judged to be in the maturity of their faculties.[120]

U. S. Mehta has written of the mentality in which 'India is a child for which the empire offers the prospect of legitimate and progressive parentage'.[121] The education of a colony is one in which the educator cannot quite believe that his charge has reached maturity. What the colonists want, perhaps subconsciously, is a response akin to that which Rousseau's Émile gave his tutor. Émile, like Mill, received a famously thorough education, although of a different sort. Rousseau writes from the perspective of the tutor rather than the pupil, and though the latter is trained for independence, the former cannot quite imagine him grasping it. Rather than being left bereft of his pupil, the tutor projects a future in which Émile is unable to discard the habits of his youth. Once married, his responsibilities daunt him. He cannot manage. He pleads to his tutor not to abandon him. This is from the final paragraph of a long book: 'Advise and control us; we shall be easily led: as long as I live I shall need you. I need you more than ever now that I am taking up the duties of manhood.'[122] Have we not here a theory of education in which Rousseau's subservient pupil, like Mill's subservient people, is moulded in the master's image, approximates to him, but cannot quite be allowed ultimately to bridge the gulf between them lest the latter's domination be forfeited?[123] Nevertheless, improvement was the essence of Mill's many writings on both individuals and societies, and it is his attitude to progress that must now concern us.

NOTES

1. A. Ferguson, *An Essay on the History of Civil Society* [1767] (Cambridge: Cambridge University Press, 1995), p. 25. Also see A. D. Smith, *The Ethnic Origin of Nations* (Oxford: Blackwell, 1986), p. 48; J. Boardman et al., *The Oxford History of the Classical World* (Oxford: Oxford University Press, 1994), pp. 40, 48, 324.
2. Montesquieu, *Spirit of the Laws* [1748] (Cambridge: Cambridge University Press, 1989), p. 234.
3. Ferguson, *Essay*, p. 108.
4. As Adam Smith in *The Theory of Moral Sentiments* [1759] (Indianapolis, IN: Liberty Fund, 1984), pp. 205–10.
5. Montesquieu, *Spirit of the Laws*, p. 290.
6. Ferguson, *Essay*, p. 81; see also p. 118.
7. Ibid., p. 99; see also pp. 229, 142, 172.

8. J. Bentham, *The Theory of Legislation* [1802] (London: Kegan Paul, 1931), p. 375. Also see pp. 109, 113, 118, 367, 369.
9. MCW, X, p. 132.
10. MCW, II, p. 164.
11. MCW, X, p. 141. Also in MCW, XX, p. 46.
12. MCW, I, p. 5.
13. 'At the very least it is odd that a strong feminist, writing under the correcting eye of an equally strong feminist, should have given himself but a single parent in the opening narrative sentence of his autobiography.' Introduction to MCW, I edited by J. M. Robson and J. Stillinger, pp. xvii–xviii.
14. James Mill, *Political Writings*, ed. T. Ball (Cambridge: Cambridge University Press, 1992), p. ix.
15. MCW, X, p. 320.
16. MCW, I, pp. 27, 29.
17. G. D. Bearce, *British Attitudes Towards India 1784–1858* (Oxford: Oxford University Press, 1961), p. 66.
18. J. J. Clarke, *Oriental Enlightenment* (London: Routledge, 1997), p. 72. Also see U. S. Mehta, *Liberalism and Empire: A Study in Nineteenth-Century British Liberal Thought* (Chicago, IL: University of Chicago Press, 1999), ch. V, 'Edmund Burke on the Perils of the Empire'.
19. Quoted in Bearce, *British Attitudes*, p. 68.
20. *On Liberty*, p. 13.
21. James Mill, *The History of British India* (London: James Maden, 1840), vol. 2., bk II, ch. x, pp. 201–2.
22. Ibid., p. 187.
23. Ibid, ch. V, pp. 516, 499.
24. Emphasis added. Ibid., bk II, ch. x, p. 187.
25. Ibid., pp. 207, 181.
26. Introduction to A. Ferguson, *Essay*, p. xxv.
27. James Mill, *History*, vol. 2., bk II, ch. x, p. 212.
28. For a markedly different and much earlier assessment, in the eleventh century the Moslem geographer Idrisi noted that 'The Indians are naturally inclined to justice, and never depart from it in their actions. Their good faith, honesty and fidelity to their engagements are well known, and they are so famous for these qualities that people flock to their country from every side.' Quoted in J. Nehru, *The Discovery of India* (New York: Doubleday, 1959), p. 142 .
29. James Mill, *History*, vol. 2, ch. V, pp. 517–18.
30. Ibid., ch. x, p. 213.
31. Ibid., pp. 219, 220.
32. Ibid., p. 214.
33. Ibid., pp. 210, 212.
34. J. Bentham, 'Essay on the Influence of Time and Place in Matters of Legislation' (1782) in *The Works of Jeremy Bentham*, pt. 1, ed. J. Bowring (Edinburgh: Tait, 1838), p. 185.
35. *History*, vol. 2, ch. V, p. 502.
36. Quoted in A. Ryan, 'Utilitarianism and Bureaucracy: The Views of J. S. Mill' in G. Sutherland (ed.), *Studies in the Growth of Nineteenth-Century Government* (London: Routledge and Kegan Paul, 1972), p. 41.

37. D. Forbes, 'James Mill and India', *Cambridge Journal*, V, 1951–52, p. 23.
38. J. E. Thorold Rogers (ed.), *Speeches on Questions of Public Policy by John Bright, M.P.* (London: Macmillan, 1869), p. 100.
39. MCW, I, p. 29.
40. L. Zastoupil, *John Stuart Mill and India* (Stanford, CA: Stanford University Press, 1994), p. 172.
41. MCW, I, p. 243.
42. See J. Plamenatz, *The English Utilitarians* (Oxford: Blackwell, 1949), p. 144; W. Donner, 'Mill's Utilitarianism' in J. Skorupski (ed.), *The Cambridge Companion to Mill* (Cambridge: Cambridge University Press, 1998), p. 255.
43. MCW, XVIII, p. 123.
44. Zastoupil, *John Stuart Mill and India*, p. 175.
45. MCW, XI, p. 290.
46. Zastoupil, *John Stuart Mill and India*, p. 85.
47. MCW, II, p. 320.
48. Quoted in Zastoupil, *John Stuart Mill and India*, p. 80.
49. Ibid., p. 97.
50. Nehru, *Discovery of India*, p. 219.
51. Quoted in Zastoupil, *John Stuart Mill and India*, p. 93.
52. MCW, II, pp. 320, 321–2.
53. MCW, XIX, p. 577.
54. *Works*, ed. Bowring, vol. 1, pp. 178–9, 187.
55. J. Bentham, 'Emancipate Your Colonies! Address to the National Convention of France, 1793, Shewing the Uselessness and Mischievousness of Distant Dependencies to an European State', in P. Shofield, C. Pease Watkin and C. Blamires (eds), *The Collected Works of Jeremy Bentham. Rights, Representation, and Reform. Nonsense Upon Stilts and Other Writings on the French Revolution* (Oxford: Clarendon Press, 2002).
56. E. Halévy, *The Growth of Philosophic Radicalism* (London: Faber & Faber, 1948), p. 510.
57. *Works*, ed. Bowring, vol. 1, p. 188.
58. Halévy, *Growth of Philosophic Radicalism*, p. 511.
59. See, for example, *The Theory of Legislation*, p. 18 and *The Principles of Morals and Legislation* [1789] (New York: Hafner, 1965), p. 267.
60. See pp. 58–9 and p. 268 fn.
61. Halévy, *Growth of Philosophic Radicalism*, p. 510.
62. *Works*, ed. Bowring, vol. 1, p. 180.
63. Quoted in Halévy, *Growth of Philosophic Radicalism*, p. 510.
64. James Mill, *Political Writings*, ed. T. Ball (Cambridge: Cambridge University Press, 1992), p. 22.
65. Thorold Rogers (ed.), *Speeches by John Bright*, p. 105.
66. A. Ryan, 'Mill and Rousseau: Utility and Rights' in G. Duncan (ed.), *Democratic Theory and Practice* (Cambridge: Cambridge University Press, 1983), p. 48.
67. A. Ryan, 'Utilitarianism and Bureaucracy: The Views of J. S. Mill', p. 40.
68. A. Bain, *James Mill: A Biography* [1882] (New York: A. M. Kelly, 1967), p. 242.
69. James Mill, *Three Articles from the Encyclopaedia Britannica* (London: J. Innes, 1824), pp. 17, 24.

70. Ibid., pp. 32, 18.
71. See MCW, XXII, p. 289.
72. *On Liberty*, pp. 13–14.
73. Ibid., p. 13.
74. *Parliamentary Papers*, 1852–53, vol. XXX, p. 313.
75. MCW, XIX, p. 419.
76. See p. 378.
77. See Nehru, *Discovery of India*, pp. 172–3.
78. Emphasis added. MCW, I, p. 177.
79. MCW, XIX, pp. 393–4.
80. E. Stokes, *The English Utilitarians and India* (Delhi: Oxford University Press, 1992), p. 65.
81. MCW, XXI, pp. 118, 119, 120.
82. Ibid., p. 118.
83. Ibid., pp. 118–19.
84. 'But what is the law of nations? Something, which to call a law at all, is a misapplication of terms. The law of nations is simply the custom of nations. It is a set of international usages, which have grown up like other usages, partly from a sense of justice, partly from common interest or convenience, partly from mere opinion and prejudice.' MCW, XX, p. 345 and see p. 346. See also the valuable discussion in G. Varouxakis, *Mill on Nationality* (London: Routledge, 2002), ch. 5, 'International Relations, Intervention/Non-intervention and National Self-determination'.
85. MCW, XXI, p. 119.
86. Ibid., p. 118.
87. Ibid., p. 119.
88. Ibid.
89. Ibid.
90. MCW, XIX, pp. 562, 568, 416.
91. MCW, XIX, p. 419.
92. Emphasis added. MCW, XIX, p. 567.
93. MCW, XXVII, p. 647.
94. See Nehru, *Discovery of India*, p. 163.
95. MCW, XIX, pp. 562, 568, 569, 570, 571, 574.
96. K. Marx and F. Engels, *Articles on Britain* (Moscow: Progress Publishers, 1975), pp. 170, 171. See also the other articles on India in this collection.
97. Emphasis added. MCW, XIX, p. 383.
98. E. Burke, *Reflections on the Revolution in France* [1790] (London: Dent, 1964), pp. 93–4.
99. Quoted in Zastoupil, *John Stuart Mill and India*, p. 97. Emphasis added.
100. Quoted in ibid., p. 111.
101. Emphasis added. T. R. Metcalf, *Ideologies of the Raj* (Cambridge: Cambridge University Press, 1994), p. 33.
102. W. Stafford, *John Stuart Mill* (Basingstoke: Macmillan, 1998), p. 109.
103. See A. P. Thornton, *Doctrines of Imperialism* (New York: Wiley, 1965).
104. 'Mill in a Liberal Landscape' in J. Skorupski (ed.), *Cambridge Companion* , p. 531.
105. A. Ryan, 'Utilitarianism and Bureaucracy: The Views of J. S. Mill', p. 41.
106. *On Liberty*, p. 14.

107. Ryan, 'Utilitarianism and Bureaucracy', p. 45.
108. MCW, XIX, p. 565.
109. MCW, XIX, pp. 561, 563.
110. MCW, XXIV, p. 880.
111. MCW, VI, p. 216.
112. MCW, VI, pp. 505–32. See also Bruce L. Kinzer, *England's Disgrace? J. S. Mill and the Irish Question* (Toronto: University of Toronto Press, 2001).
113. See MCW, XXIV, pp. 879–1035, 1066–78, and M. Levin, *The Condition of England Question: Carlyle, Mill, Engels* (Basingstoke: Macmillan, 1998), pp. 90–6.
114. See MCW, XX, pp. 317–63 and M. Levin, *Condition of England Question*, pp. 111–15.
115. See particularly MCW, II, pp. 199–214, MCW, III, pp. 975–87.
116. See MCW, I, pp. 280–2 and Packe, *Life of Mill* , pp. 465–72.
117. MCW, XXI, pp. 259–340 and also included in the edition which I have used here for references to *On Liberty*, that is J. S. Mill, *On Liberty and Other Writings*, ed. S. Collini (Cambridge, 1989), pp. 117–217.
118. See U. S. Mehta, *Liberalism and Empire: A Study in Nineteenth-Century British Liberal Thought* (Chicago, IL: University of Chicago Press, 1999).
119. See I. Berlin, *The First and the Last* (London: Granta Books, 1999), pp. 74–8.
120. Mill, *On Liberty*, p. 14.
121. U. S. Mehta, *Liberalism and Empire*, p. 32.
122. J. J. Rousseau, *Émile* [1762] (London: Dent, 1963), p. 444.
123. For Britain's economic motives in holding on to India, see E. J. Hobsbawm, *Industry and Empire* (Harmondsworth: Penguin Books, 1969), p. 149.

Chapter Four

Progress

FROM BARBARISM TO CIVILIZATION

A key question concerning Mill's theory of civilization as a process is how some peoples find their own means of advancement and others don't. It was clearly no small achievement to have ascended the ladder of development, for 'few nations have ever attained at all, and still fewer by their own independent development, a high state of social progress'.[1] How, then, did Britain advance to its current heights? Was it an autonomous process or through the benefit of foreign invasion? It seems plausible to accept that the Romans brought civilization to Britain, but they came and then, a few centuries later, went. Another civilizing influence would be that of the Normans, who came and stayed. It might have rather pleased Mill to think of Britain becoming civilized through the French. This raises the problem of infinite regress, however, for how then did the Normans rise from barbarism? Did they have their own Akbar and, if so, from which society did he come? Progress could not originally have been brought from the outside, so how did it start?

Before asking how a society develops, however, we must, in this instance, ponder how it is formed in the first place. For some theorists this is not an issue. For a tradition that probably commences with Aristotle and continues through to Burke, Marx and Durkheim, society came first. Mankind is naturally social. The group, whether in the form of family, clan, tribe or *ethnie*, is natural. In Durkheim's theory of development, for instance, the initial stage of mechanical solidarity was one where human similarity predominated. Each society started as a monochrome mass and gradually, through the increasing division of labour, became more differentiated. Increasing individuality, then, was the result of a protracted historical process; it was a social product. The contrast with Mill is quite striking. He was not a social contract theorist in the seventeenth- and eighteenth-century sense, but he inherited that liberal tradition which took individuality as primary in both an ethical and a historical sense. For him the individual came first. The pre-social individual had to be persuaded or coerced into society and only then, with a stable, intact union, could the long journey to civilization continue.

So, how, then, did progress start? What qualities and situations were necessary? In his essay on 'Coleridge' Mill noted that the 'very first element of the social union, obedience to a government of some sort, has not been found so easy a thing to establish in the world'.[2] Mill was an advocate of both freedom and civilization. He assumed that freedom came before civilization and was initially diminished by it. Mill could have echoed Rousseau that man was born free, though not that he was everywhere in chains. The first step of civilization, ironically, was to subdue that freedom. How, then, were free individuals persuaded to surrender their autonomy? Mill again almost echoes Rousseau's structure of thought in the *Discourse on Inequality* by regarding trickery as the device by which a social union was attained. For Rousseau the trickery was that of the rich against the poor, pretending to guard the weak while actually fortifying the property of the strong. For Mill, in contrast, society as such was not viewed unfavourably; it had not been a mistake to establish it. The trickery lay in the mode of persuasion, religion being used as a kind of noble lie. He seems to divide pre-social mankind into two 'races'. The first were 'timid and spiritless ... like the inhabitants of the vast plains of tropical countries'. Here Mill thought 'passive obedience may be of natural growth', but then he immediately modified that generalization with the limitation that it probably never applied except where 'fatalism, or in other words, submission to the pressure of circumstances as the decree of God, did not prevail as a religious doctrine'. For a 'brave and warlike race' religion was also necessary. Only the presumption of 'supernatural power', that is the attribution of civil society to a 'divine origin', could have been enough to persuade such people to submit themselves to a 'common umpire'.[3]

In the 'Coleridge' essay Mill did not tackle the question of why free individuals might submit themselves to the disciplines of society. What imperative provided the motive for such a transformation? An approximate answer came twenty years later in the *Considerations on Representative Government*. Here Mill mentioned that 'the first lesson of civilization' was 'that of obedience' and that it was usually achieved 'through the necessities of warfare, and the despotic authority indispensable to military command'. This is only an approximate answer, because Mill here assumed warfare between tribes, which are presumably social units, however rudimentary, for he also mentioned their 'turbulent insubordination' and 'savage independence'.[4] War, then, if not the first moment of social union, seems to be placed very shortly thereafter.

It seems that war develops a people or destroys them. A tribe that fails in the challenge of war is subsumed into the society of its conquerors, whereas one that meets the challenge, through creating structures of authority and obedience, has taken the essential next step on the ladder of civilization. But war can take a people only so far. One step need not lead to another unless further prerequisites, even more demanding and rare, are attained. This brings us to Mill's emphasis on mental activity.

Mill's own personal advancement was secured by a prodigious educational process. What had worked for him as an individual had also assisted societies. *Initial* survival required physical qualities; *further* advance required mental ones and the focus on education was ubiquitous in Mill's writings. In the *Logic* Mill noted that 'speculation, intellectual activity, the pursuit of truth ... is the main determining cause of the social progress' and that every 'considerable advance in material civilization has been preceded by an advance in knowledge'.[5] In *The Principles of Political Economy* Mill's focus was obviously more on material and productive development. A useful motive here was sheer hardship, for it produces the qualities that lead to greater productivity and development. Mill noted that 'it is difficulties, not facilities, that nourish bodily and mental energy'. In the early stages of development, the tribes that were more successful were those 'mostly reared amidst hardship'. Where sustenance may be had with little effort the motive to be energetic was too slight. For this reason 'military vigour, as well as speculative thought and industrial energy, have all had their principal seats in the less favoured North'. The problem with this general theory was that it obviously failed to account for the early emergence of Western civilization in ancient Greece and Rome. Mill's response was not particularly convincing: in Greece and Rome the absence of 'natural hardships' was replaced by the presumably equally beneficial 'artificial ones of a rigid military discipline'.[6] The same mentality is also present in some of Mill's comments on the British aristocracy. They, like the savages of southern climes, were having it too easy, and not having to exert themselves was doing them no good. In a letter to John Austin, Mill noted that the 'English higher classes' suffered a 'total absence of the habit of exerting their minds for any purpose whatever'. He concluded that the 'more the path to any meritorious attainment is made smooth to an individual or a class, from their early youth, the less chance there is of their realizing it. Never to have had any difficulties to overcome seems fatal to mental vigour.'[7] We might just add here that the emphasis on the virtues of hardship seems scarcely compatible with the utilitarian pursuit of happiness and in the above comments Mill's seems much closer to the very arguments Thomas Carlyle used to oppose utilitarianism.[8]

Early development was also attributed to the propensity to save, a disposition which varied immensely from one people to another and which was fundamental in determining their chances of development. Mill believed that 'Individuals and communities of a very low state of *intelligence* are always improvident. A certain measure of *intellectual development* seems necessary to enable absent things, and especially things future, to act with any force on the imagination and will.'[9] It seemed that peoples did not differ particularly in the amount of work they were prepared to do but in – what is a mental attribute – 'their capacity of present exertion for a distant object'. The North American Indians exerted great efforts when strictly necessary, yet their 'indolence is proverbial'. So, to 'civilize a savage' requires that he be 'inspired with new wants and desires' of a kind that require continuous labour. Mill noted that 'the negroes of Jamaica and Demerara' were induced to work by 'their love of fine clothes and personal ornaments'.[10] This was not a tendency that Mill encouraged in more advanced societies, but in an early stage of development it could clearly have positive consequences in developing a habit of work.

In *Representative Government* Mill asked what are 'the particular attributes in human beings which seem to have a more especial reference to Progress'. Unsurprisingly, he instanced 'mental activity, enterprise, and courage'. He also noted that the 'mental attribute which seems exclusively dedicated to Progress, and is the culmination of the tendencies to it, is Originality, or Invention'.[11]

We have outlined the attributes that were necessary for progress and so should now turn to Mill's conjectures on where it actually commenced. In his *Autobiography* Mill wrote: 'I have no remembrance of the time when I began to learn Greek; I have been told that it was when I was three years old.'[12] So Greek came first in Mill's education just as the Greeks had themselves come first in achieving civilization. In an 1846 review of his friend George Grote's *History of Greece* Mill declared that 'they *alone* among nations, so far as is known to us, emerged from barbarism by their own efforts, not following in the track of any more advanced people'.[13] In Mill's time knowledge of the classics was, of course, a fundamental attribute of the educated person. Apart from the mental discipline of acquiring classical languages, the histories of ancient Greece and Rome, the causes of both their rise and fall, were taken as providing examples and precepts for the guidance of all later generations. For Mill,

> history points out no other people in the ancient world who had any spring of unborrowed progress within themselves. We have no knowledge of any other source from which freedom and intellectual cultivation could have come, any other means by which the light never since extinguished might have been kindled, if the world had been left, without any elements of Grecian origin.[14]

The first modification of this view came four years later in 'The Negro Question', Mill's principled response to Carlyle's less delicately titled diatribe on 'The Nigger Question'. Mill declared it 'curious withal, that the earliest known civilization was … a negro civilization'. From their sculptures he presumed that the ancient Egyptians were black. 'It was from negroes, therefore, that the Greeks learnt their first lessons in civilization.'[15] This was, of course, a powerful counter to Carlyle's racism. It contains also a very rare instance of Mill explicitly viewing civilization in the plural and explicitly referring to any ancient culture as a civilization, a label he was never willing to apply to the sophisticated cultures of India.[16] Our question, then, recurs in respect of the Egyptians. Was their civilization indigenous and, if so, from what qualities and circumstances did it emerge? If it was not indigenous, who, then, was their provider, their Akbar or Charlemagne?

A further modification may be found in Chapter Two of *Representative Government*. Here Mill pointed out that in China and Egypt despotism had provided 'fit instruments for carrying those nations up to the point of civilization which they attained. But having reached that point, they were brought to a permanent halt for want of mental liberty and individuality.' For that reason, 'further improvement stopped'. Mill then turned to 'a comparatively insignificant Oriental people – the Jews'. In stark and significant contrast to the Chinese and Egyptians, 'neither their kings nor their priests ever obtained ... the exclusive moulding of their character'. The Jewish prophets 'kept up, in that little corner of the earth, the antagonism of influences which is the only real security for continued progress'. In this particular instance religion 'was not there, what it has been in so many other places – a consecration of all that was once established, and a barrier against further improvement'. The structure of pluralism was such that 'Conditions more favourable to Progress could not easily exist: accordingly, the Jews, instead of being stationary like other Asiatics, were, next to the Greeks, the most progressive people of antiquity, and, jointly with them, have been the *starting-point and main propelling agency* of modern cultivation.'[17]

For Mill, then, modern civilization derived from Jewish and Greek origins, two cultures that both valued intellectual activity and gave it the space to flourish. Their particular power structures had facilitated a pluralism that had made progress possible. There seems to have been no plan to encourage development; rather was it a case of fortuitous good luck, and rare good luck at that, for no other cultures seem to have been so fortunate. According to Stefan Collini, the thinkers of Mill's time characteristically regarded progress as 'very much the exception. The great empires of the east had, like the indigenous civilisations in most parts of the world, remained essentially static.'[18] Mill himself noted that the stationary 'condition is far more congenial to ordinary human nature' than the progressive[19] and that therefore 'among the inhabitants of our earth, the European family of nations is the only one which has ever yet shown any capability of spontaneous improvement, beyond a certain low level'.[20] Mill, then, shared with Tocqueville, Marx and just about every other major Western thinker of his time, a strong belief in European pre-eminence. For example, his contemporary Arthur de Gobineau wrote on the difficulties of making the first step of civilization: 'Indeed, the human species seems to have a very great difficulty in raising itself above a rudimentary type of organization; the transition to a more complex state is made only by those groups or tribes that are eminently gifted.'[21] In his work on *Ancient Law*, published in 1861, Sir Henry Maine explained that civilization was western European. He noted that societies could be classified as stationary or progressive and that nothing was 'more remarkable' than the 'extreme fewness' of the latter. The 'stationary condition of the human race is the rule, the progressive the exception'.[22] Walter Bagehot believed that 'As a rule ... a stationary state is by far the most frequent condition of man ... the progressive state is only a rare and an occasional exception.'[23] For such people the various known societies around the globe could be arranged according to their fairly self-evident place in the hierarchy that led slowly upwards from barbarism to civilization. There were civilized Europeans on the one side and barbarians on the other and only the influence of the former could elevate the latter. For a sense of the distance involved we can mention Charles Darwin, who did 'not believe it possible to describe or paint the difference between savage and civilized man. It is the difference between a wild and tame animal.'[24] No society, then, was born civilized or possessed it by divine right. Civilization was an achievement of the West that had been hard won and had come at a late stage of a long process.

The attempt to delineate a precise sequence of human advance was first developed significantly by the thinkers of the Scottish Enlightenment.[25] A further step in that direction had been taken in the 1790s by Condorcet, whose *Sketch of a Historical Picture of the Progress of the Human Mind* set the tone for much later French thought in this area. Mill acknowledged that following his mental crisis the main immediate influence on him was that of the Saint-Simonians. He recalled being 'greatly struck with the connected view which they for the first time presented to me, of the natural order of human progress; and especially with their division of all history into organic periods and critical periods'.[26] From out of the Saint-Simonian school emerged Auguste Comte, with whom Mill had an intense but fairly brief correspondence during the 1840s.[27] Mill fell out with Comte over the latter's views on female inferiority and cannot have felt at ease with his arrogant and total self-assurance, yet remained impressed with his delineation of humanity advancing through theological, metaphysical and positivist stages. Mill, at a minimum, was concerned with the same intellectual issues as Comte. In his *System of Logic* Mill expressed it as follows: 'The fundamental problem, therefore, of the social sciences, is to find the laws according to which any state of society produces the state which succeeds it and takes its place. This opens the great and vexed question of the progressiveness of man and society.'[28]

In 1865, eight years after Comte's death, Mill attempted a résumé of his writings. While not ignoring the farcical and potentially tyrannical aspects of Comte's new religion, Mill was as benign as even-handedness permits and concluded that 'the history of our species, looked at as a comprehensive whole, does exhibit a determinate course, a certain order of development'.[29]

67

Where, however, does an order of development lead? We have thus far been concerned with the sequence by which a section of mankind advanced from barbarism to civilization. If there were a law according to which this development occurred, then, presumably, society would still be within its dictates. Perhaps, then, the logic by which mankind reached its present stage conditions or indicates the direction in which it is moving, if not the destiny to which it is ineluctably drawn?

It should by now be clear that Mill shared the characteristic nineteenth-century focus on social progress. The year 1859 that saw the publication of Mill's *On Liberty* was also the year of publication of two other highly significant works containing theories of progress, Charles Darwin's *On the Origin of Species* and Karl Marx's very brief but still highly influential 'Preface to a Critique of Political Economy', which outlined the path of development through 'Asiatic, ancient, feudal, and modern bourgeois modes of production'.[30] Like Marx, Mill was concerned to discover where society was going and what were its dynamics. Unlike him, however, he had no teleological notion of a final destination or inevitable historical course, for 'human affairs are not entirely governed by mechanical laws'.[31] Theorists of progress may be divided into determinists and voluntarists. For the former, of whom Marx is the most obvious example, the future course is inevitable. In a sociological variant of Calvinism, the working class was declared predestined to refashion society according to its presumed needs. The proletariat was riding the locomotive of history; the Onward March of Labour was as clearly on track as the passengers on the Stockton to Darlington railway line. For thinkers like Mill this mentality left too little to human choice and took insufficient account of both human history and fallibility. For Mill the future was open. Further progress was definitely possible but, as in the past, it would still have to be won the hard way; against all the vested interests who were content with how things were, and against the vast mass of intellectual indolence which had neither the imagination or intelligence to envisage improvement nor the vigour to pursue it. History certainly provided opportunities, but for Mill it gave no guarantees.

Mill's historical sense is not usually given adequate recognition, but as much as Burke and Carlyle, he was aware that society had come a very long way; and even more than Marx he also believed that it still had much further to go. Both these aspects are nicely captured in his 1850 essay on 'The Negro Question'. Here Mill noted: 'The history of human improvement is the record of a struggle by which inch after inch of ground has been wrung from these maleficent powers, and more and more of human life rescued from the iniquitous dominion of the law of might. Much, very much of this work still remains to do.'[32] Mill not infrequently seemed to view mankind from rather Olympian heights, noting 'the backward state in which speculation on the most important subjects still lingers' and also 'the comparatively early state of human advancement in which we now live'.[33] This is clearly a change of emphasis from the more Benthamite and Enlightenment view that celebrated how much was known and how advanced current thinking was. From Condorcet, Paine and Priestley, through to Marx, most social optimists tended to regard the ultimate stage as the next one, just one heave of exertion away.

THE FUTURE

Unlike the socialists, both 'scientific' and 'utopian', Mill was not into framing blueprints for future society, yet like them he did believe that civilization was not merely to be celebrated but also defended, fortified and advanced. As for the direction or content of advance, where others had plans Mill had ideals, which can be found scattered throughout his writings, and to which we now turn.

Whether these ideals are consistent is an issue we shall soon be able to judge. Chapter Five of Mill's *Autobiography* deals, retrospectively of course, with the 1826–32 period. Of that time he wrote:

> I looked forward ... to a future which shall unite the best qualities of the criti-
> cal with the best qualities of the organic periods; unchecked liberty of thought,
> unbounded freedom of individual action in all modes not hurtful to others; but
> also, convictions as to what is right and wrong, useful and pernicious, deeply
> engraven on the feelings by early education and general unanimity of sentiment,
> and so firmly grounded in reason and in the true exigencies of life that they shall
> not, like all former and present creeds, religious, ethical, and political, require to
> be periodically thrown off and replaced by others.[34]

Under the influence of the Saint-Simonians and Comte this is perhaps the closest Mill came to expressing the notion of a closed ideal, an end-state where reason has been discovered and so beliefs are static and unchallenged. Such a situation is suggestive of the Chinese stationary state that Mill was to condemn in *On Liberty*. It is, then, very much the opposite of the dominant mentality of his later years. Nevertheless it does express one side of a dualism that was to remain with him. Note that even within this one, admittedly rather long, sentence Mill combined 'unchecked liberty of thought' with general unanimity concerning what is right and wrong in matters 'religious, ethical and political'. The obvious response as Mill, in other places, was quite aware, is that a society allowing full liberty of thought is most unlikely to produce unanimity in its conclusions. It was in his essay on 'Auguste Comte and Positivism' that Mill most clearly rejected the vision of a society where the rulers declare that they know best and so can do the thinking for everyone else. Here Mill felt 'appalled at the picture of entire subjugation and slavery,

69

which is recommended to us as the last and highest result of the evolution of Humanity'.[35] Even in *On Liberty* it is not quite clear whether freedom is seen as a means or an end. In those places where Mill argues for freedom as a means of attaining truth, it does leave open the question of whether liberty is still necessary, or still as necessary, once truth is attained.

In *Principles of Political Economy* the content of progress was, perhaps appropriately, presented in more commercial terms. Here wealth augmentation and population growth equal or lead to progress, which is marked by the 'unlimited growth of man's power over nature'; a 'continual increase of the security of person and property'; better protection 'against arbitrary exercise of the power of government ... a great increase both of production and of accumulation' and 'an improvement in the business capacities of the general mass of mankind' and 'the capacity of co-operation'.[36] Thus far this seems to intimate the continuation of things as they were. Like Marx and Tocqueville, however, Mill realized that modern civilization was a mixed blessing and, for a supposedly 'classic' or archetypal liberal, he was unusually critical of the commercial ethos. As is well known, in *Political Economy* he actually recommended a form of 'standstill' – the stationary state. This, it must be strongly emphasized, is *not* the same stationary state that Mill found in China and feared in the West, for the type that he recommended was one in which *only* the level of capital and population need be at a standstill. Other social developments could and would continue unabated. Its stationariness, then, was partial, an economic standstill that was intended to facilitate a flourishing of the wider culture. This condition was very far from mass society and the tyranny of the majority for it facilitated a flowering of intellectual endeavour. 'There would be as much scope as ever for all kinds of mental culture, and moral and social progress.'[37]

In *On Liberty* Mill's ideal was one of the full unfolding of personal capacities. He quoted approvingly from von Humboldt that the 'end of man ... is the highest and most harmonious development of his powers to a complete and consistent whole'.[38]

In Bentham's formulation, utilitarianism was a creed which advocated the greatest happiness of the greatest number by means of all individuals pursuing their own personal happiness. His *Fragment on Government* was first published in 1776, the same year as Adam Smith's *The Wealth of Nations*, and it seems to share part of the same mentality. For Smith an invisible guiding hand was conveniently available to harmonize the individual pursuit of self-interest with the collective interest of the society. Bentham has no such explicit mechanism but like Smith still assumed that individual and collective aspirations would naturally harmonize. Bentham also assumed that human nature was one and the same everywhere, with all individuals pursuing happiness and avoiding pain; in other words, utilitarianism was part of our nature. If this were so, one might ask why we need the propagation of a creed to encourage us at what we do anyway. Bentham's answer was that mankind was not sufficiently conscious of its underlying motivations and that proper awareness could produce the more complete achievement of utilitarian aims. The obvious implication of this, though Bentham did not rigorously pursue it, is that human society could be considerably improved.

This brings us back to Mill. Mill is sometimes seen as a subverter of the utilitarian creed, with his two critical commentaries on Bentham, and his *On Liberty* seen by some critics, most notably by Sir Isaiah Berlin, as substantially devoid of the utilitarian spirit.[39] In *Utilitarianism*, however, Mill faced the difficult problem, which Bentham left aside, of how individual and general needs could be reconciled. It was just such a reconciliation that for Mill formed part of his image of the future.

With government comes control, and for Mill society was still in the relatively early stage where the utilitarian morality required the sanction of law. There were still people who would not voluntarily obey any system of morality and for them sanctions were necessary. Mill outlined two kinds of sanctions, external and internal. The external ones consist of both the law, in its most visible presence of the policeman, and also the pressures applied by society. The internal sanction is that of conscience. Mill implied that in time the external sanction could be reduced as people become increasingly conscientious, leading to a state of affairs where they would identify more completely with the community. This 'natural tendency' is reinforced by becoming transformed into an ideological replacement for religion.

> If we now suppose this feeling of unity to be taught as a religion, and the whole force of education, of institutions, and of opinion, directed, as it once was in the case of religion, to make every person grow up from infancy surrounded on all sides both by the profession and by the practice of it, I think that no one, who can realize this conception, will feel any misgiving about the sufficiency of the ultimate sanction for the Happiness morality.[40]

The pursuit of unity and the assertion of a common human nature were part of the characteristic radical mindset. In the same way, if we may generalise, radicals have often been centralizers and conservatives decentralizers. Radicals want uniformity and conservatives defend difference. In Mill, who grappled to combine what seemed most plausible in both Bentham and Coleridge, we find aspects of both mentalities. English liberals from Hume onwards have tended to believe in a common human nature, and some from Paine onwards have believed in universal human rights, yet these aspects of sameness have often been combined with a belief in the benefits of pluralism. In *On Liberty* Mill expressed the pure liberal creed of diversity and decried the adverse effects of advancing similarity. Sameness was very much the enemy, as we shall see in the following chapters. Yet just a few years later in

71

Utilitarianism he looked forward to increasing unity, noting that in 'an improving state of the human mind, the influences are constantly on the increase, which tend to generate in each individual a feeling of unity with all the rest'. He welcomed 'the desire to be in unity with our fellow creatures ... as mankind are further removed from the state of savage independence'.[41] The pursuit of harmony is characteristically a component of a left-wing utopia and is associated with a fairly equal society. Mill wanted both difference and unity. It would be a difficult balancing act, for it is not clear how, outside of major dangers such as war, an unequal and variegated society can generate the degree of solidarity that the term 'unity' seems to imply. In *Utilitarianism* we also find one of Mill's most optimistic and utopian statements, for he declared 'that most of the great positive evils of the world are in themselves removable', including poverty, which may be 'completely extinguished'.[42]

In his *Autobiography* Mill explained how he achieved 'a greater approximation, so far as regards the ultimate prospects of humanity, to a qualified Socialism',[43] unfortunately here failing to specify precisely what the qualifications were. Otherwise the most favourable account of socialism he published in his lifetime is usually taken to be the chapter 'On the Probable Futurity of the Labouring Classes', published in Book Four of *Principles of Political Economy*. This chapter is said to have been included on the advice, or on the insistence, of Harriet Taylor and so is, perhaps, for some not fully convincing as an expression of Mill's authentic opinions. We have seen, however, that there are parts of *Utilitarianism* which also express a whole number of sentiments shared with the socialists.

What one editor of Mill's writings has noted as his 'first major comments on labour'[44] appeared in his 1845 review of *The Claims of Labour: An Essay on the Duties of the Employers to the Employed* by Arthur Helps. Here Mill noted that from the time of Malthus 'the economical condition of the labouring classes [had] been regarded by thoughtful men as susceptible of permanent improvement' yet such improvement had not obviously occurred. According to Mill, the Chartist movement 'was the first open separation of interest, feeling, and opinion, between the labouring portion of the commonwealth and all above them'. One way or another it was a symptom of a bad situation. Its emergence indicated that in some respects working-class complaints were justified, for Mill declared the labourer 'a mere bought instrument in the work of production, having no residuary interest in the work itself'. To overcome this situation required that workers be granted a degree of partnership in their employment by means of 'a commission on the returns instead of only a fixed salary'.[45] Mill's co-option of the workers into profit sharing was intended to reduce the class divide while still leaving the capitalists, and now their 'teams', competing against each other.

Similar concerns were expressed three years later in *Political Economy*. Here Mill noted that, in contrast to America and Australia, in England the division into employers and employed was almost hereditary. Those who began life as hired labourers hardly ever escaped from that condition. Class relations seemed frozen and there was a 'standing feud between capital and labour'.[46] Beyond getting their wages, workers had no further interest in the enterprise that employed them.

What, then, should be done about the condition of the working class? Mill favoured their trade-union activity as a means by which they could defend their position. He also, as ever, recommended more education so as to advance the rationality of their actions. This, he hoped, would lead to them having fewer children, as those unable to care for their dependants become themselves dependent on others. Dependency for Mill was one part of a power relationship and therefore dependent people lose their autonomy and hence their freedom. Mill also wanted improved relations between the classes; 'a friendly rivalry in the pursuit of a good common to all'.[47] Further, as noted in the 1845 review, Mill recommended profit sharing under the owners' management as a means of integrating workers into capitalist enterprises.

From one perspective profit sharing was a means of integrating the working classes into the capitalist enterprise; from another, it seemed a step towards socialism itself. While Mill was writing *Political Economy*, socialist movements were emerging in France, England and Germany, and Mill commented on what seemed to be the two most popular forms. What Mill then called 'communism' was not the movement currently being established by Marx and Engels, of whom he had not heard. It consisted, rather, of Owen, Louis Blanc, Cabet and their respective followers. These people allegedly believed in absolute equality of distribution. Mill rejected their belief in compulsory alternating labour, which he thought would diminish productivity and also feared that they could 'renounce liberty for the sake of equality'.[48]

Mill's second category, that of socialism, described those who allowed for some inequality, but based it on the application of a recognized principle, such as that of justice, rather than on random chance. The most reputable socialist theories were held to be those of Saint-Simon and Fourier. Mill thought Saint-Simonian socialism was one step better than communism but Fourierism was more advanced still. It removed neither private property nor inheritance. Individualism was fostered rather than suppressed and the incentive for ambition was retained. Full communal living was rejected, although all members were expected to live in the same group of buildings. The socialism of the scheme consisted of labour being communally organized. The community was to be divided into social groups formed by self-affiliation. Individuals could belong to more than one group and change their membership at will.

In Fourierism, democracy is more conspicuous than in Owenism and Saint-Simonism, for the sharp division between management, however rational and benevolent, and ordinary membership has been overcome. In

73

Fourier's plan there was a minimum subsistence level automatically granted to all, whether they laboured or not. Beyond that individual votes would determine the remuneration that particular people receive and so all members would have an incentive to develop their skills and make themselves useful to the community.

The assumed level of public spirit and self-restraint is clearly considerable and Mill was well aware of the educational and moral prerequisites. In a low state of human development such a system could produce jealousies that threatened the whole enterprise. What was required was 'a degree of disinterestedness and of freedom from vanity' currently 'only found in the élite of humanity'. The elite, however, were a vanguard. What was possible for them would in the future and with the advance of education, become so for all. Furthermore a scheme considered only in terms of a single community would be required to expand to 'the whole industry of a nation, and even of the world'![49] Fourier's had clearly produced a brand of socialism that, more than most, could appeal to the liberal disposition. Mill ends his account, however, by treating it as a vision for the future rather than a policy for the present.

The Principles of Political Economy was finished and went into press in December 1847. The first of seven editions was published in April 1848. Between those dates, of course, revolution broke out in Paris and many of the other major European cities. Mill, where possible and plausible, liked to use the French example as a stick with which to beat British recalcitrance, and so played Paine to Lord Brougham's Burke in writing a spirited 'Vindication of the French Revolution of February 1848'. Now with radicalism so clearly at the top of the agenda, Mill took a more optimistic stance on socialism than he had just a year earlier. It now seemed 'a perfectly just demand ... that the government should aid with its funds, to a reasonable extent, in bringing into operation industrial communities on the Socialist principle'.[50]

Mill's most explicit avowal of socialism is found in the last chapter of his *Autobiography*. Here he decided that his 'ideal of ultimate improvement ... would class us decidedly under the general designation of Socialists.' Though he rejected

> that tyranny of society over the individual which most Socialistic systems are supposed to involve, we yet looked forward to a time when society will no longer be divided into the idle and the industrious; when the rule that they who do not work shall not eat, will be applied not to paupers only, but impartially to all; when the division of the produce of labour, instead of depending, as in so great a degree it now does, on the accident of birth, will be made by concert on an acknowledged principle of justice.[51]

Mill's last words on socialism were written in 1869 but not published until 1879, six years after his death. By his later years Mill had become aware of not just township or community socialism but of projects for taking over a whole country. Of this aspect, he clearly rejected revolution, decided that communist management would not be innovative, feared that private life would be subject to greater public control and rejected the idea that a whole industry could be directed from a single centre. Mill welcomed the co-operative aspect of the socialist mentality but rejected the socialist opposition to competition. A co-operating team has to have other teams to compete against. If all of society co-operated with itself monopolies would emerge and go sluggish through lack of competitive edge. Though Mill thought that the benefits that were most plausible under socialism could also be obtained under a more developed system of private property, he remained to the end open-minded enough to call for practical experiments to demonstrate the viability of communism.

A NOTE ON ANTIQUITY

A believer in unilinear progress would be committed to the view of the later the better, the earlier the worse. Time would be the measure of improvement. Earlier in time would indicate lesser development; later in time, greater development. If the classics were held – as indeed they sometimes were – to embody timeless profundities, then the societies from which they emerged presumably still had something to teach us. This ruled out any facile notion that early necessarily implied primitive.

A simple notion of unilinear progress has to denigrate ancient cultures. This was certainly apparent in both Mills' writings on India. It was indeed part of the culture of both utilitarianism and the Enlightenment more generally. Mill himself noted that the 'disrespect in which history was held by the *philosophes* is notorious; one of the soberest of them, D'Alembert we believe, was the author of the wish that all record whatever of past events could be blotted out'.[52]

However, the counter-Enlightenment rejected the notion that one singular, contemporary, rationalist view could adequately stratify diverse and distant societies according to its own standard. It also denied that the present was always an improvement on the past and tended to see in the middle ages an ideal of community solidarity and Christian authority that modernity had fatally undermined. The Romantics further valued the uniqueness of each culture as having its own particular worth and authenticity. Mill came near to this broader view, appropriately enough, in his essay on 'Coleridge'. Here, he noted:

> human nature had exhibited many of its noblest manifestations, not in Christian countries only, but in the ancient world, in Athens, Sparta, Rome; nay, even

75

barbarians, as the Germans, or still more unmitigated savages, the wild Indians and again the Chinese, the Egyptians, the Arabs, all had their own education, their own culture; a culture which, whatever might be its tendency upon the whole, had been successful in some respect or other.[53]

Note that here we have greater praise for the quality of human nature in certain early non-Christian cultures than for the achievements of those societies as a whole. A moment's reflection, not to mention a visit to the British Museum or the Louvre, will confirm that 'successful in some respect or other' scarcely does justice to their considerable achievements. The 'wild Indians' are presumably Native Americans. Thus Mill avoided including India in his list of significant cultures.

Mill acknowledged his debt to the 'Germano-Coleridgian school' for aiding his appreciation of the breadth of human culture. As we know, there was one early people of whom he had prior knowledge. When he was seven he read some 'Greek prose authors, among whom I remember the whole of Herodotus, and of Xenophon's *Cyropaedia* and *Memorials of Socrates*; some of the lives of the philosophers by Diogenes Laërtius, part of Lucian, and Isocrates *Ad Demonicum* and *Ad Nicolem* in addition to six dialogues of Plato'.[54]

In the third of his 'Spirit of the Age' articles Mill referred to Athens as 'the source of light and civilization to the world, and the most inspiring and elevating example which history has yet produced, of how much human nature is capable'. Much the same was true of Rome 'as certainly demonstrated, by the steady unintermitted progress of that community from the smallest beginnings to the highest prosperity and power'.[55] This, of course, is high praise, but praise of potential, of capacity but not of ultimate development.

Perhaps Mill's most unequivocal appreciation of ancient Athens is found in his 1832 essay 'On Genius'. Here he noted that the small city state produced 'two vast intellects ... the one the greatest observer of his or any age, the other the greatest dialectician, and both almost unrivalled in their powers of metaphysical analysis – Aristotle and Plato'. Since their time education had become mere cramming, so that 'in almost every branch of literature and art we are deplorably behind the earlier ages of the world'. Anything but progress seemed to be evident, for Mill, at this stage, believed that the 'ten centuries of England and France cannot produce as many illustrious names as the hundred and fifty years of little Greece'.[56] Eugenio Biagini has noted that classical Athens was 'an unparalleled model' for Mill.[57] If so, it did not quite remain so. It seems that in 1831 and 1832 Mill voiced higher praise of ancient Athens than ever again.

Between 1846 and 1853 Mill reviewed parts of the twelve-volume *History of Greece* written by his friend George Grote. Mill believed that the Greeks were 'the most remarkable people who have yet existed ... the originators of political freedom, and the grand exemplars and sources of it to modern Europe'. Their debates 'formed a course of political education the equivalent of which modern nations have not known how to give even to those whom they educate for statesmen'.[58] Pericles himself combined positive qualities to an extent rarely seen since. In fact the Athenians were 'the most gifted community of human beings which the world has yet seen ... the light of the world from that time to this'.[59]

Their achievement, however, was one of inaugurating freedom and development rather than completing it. Certainly after 1832 Mill viewed ancient Athens as 'favourable to progress'[60] rather than the most exalted society ever. He noted that 'in several things' such as slavery and the treatment of women 'they were but few removes from barbarism' and 'radically *inferior* to the best ... products of modern civilization'. Mill found in Grote's *History*, then, ' the budding, the blossoming, and the decay and death'.[61] Clearly a civilization could emerge, rise and fall, but in the reviews Mill did not examine the latter. It seems that Mill's admiration of ancient Athens was not theorized in terms of his interest in the full pattern and logic of history. Development was a possibility, an aspiration, but definitely not a certainty. Intermittently in his reviews of Grote Mill expressed disappointment that the civic culture of ancient Athens was not being matched in his own time. Our main point, however, is that praise for the high qualities of the Athenian state undermines a simple, unilinear theory of development. Additionally Mill hardly dealt with the collapse of ancient civilizations, for some a dreadful warning for their successors. It is, then, to the weaknesses of modern civilization that we must now turn.

NOTES

1. MCW,VIII, p. 917.
2. MCW, X, p. 132.
3. Ibid.
4. MCW, XIX, p. 415.
5. MCW, VIII, pp. 926, 927.
6. MCW, II, p. 103,
7. MCW, XIII, pp. 712–13.
8. 'They wrong man greatly who say he is to be seduced by ease. Difficulty, abnegation, martyrdom, death are the *allurements* that act on the heart of man ... Not happiness, but something higher.' T. Carlyle, *On Heroes and Hero-Worship* [1841] (London: Oxford University Press, 1974), p. 93.
9. Emphasis added. MCW, II, pp. 163–4.
10. Ibid., pp. 103, 104.
11. MCW, XIX, pp. 35–6. Mill's idiosyncratic use of capitals is illuminating. As with

'Originality', 'Invention', 'Progress', the 'One' and the 'Few', capitals within a sentence are nearly always a mark of special approval.

12. MCW, I, p. 9.
13. Emphasis added. MCW, XI, p. 273.
14. MCW, XI, p. 313.
15. MCW, XXI, p. 93. This issue, of course, has been the subject of heated debate following the publication of Martin Bernal's *Black Athena. The Afroasiatic Roots of Classical Civilization*, 2 vols (London: Free Association Books, 1987, 1991). See the comments in R. J. Evans, *In Defence of History* (London: Granta Books, 1997), pp. 221–2.
16. In the 1845 article on Guizot, Mill wrote of 'the *civilizations* of the ancient world'. Emphasis added. Also of 'Roman civilization' and 'parts of the earth which were much earlier civilized' than Europe. MCW, XX, pp. 269, 271, 289.
17. Emphasis added. MCW, XIX, pp. 396–7.
18. Introduction to J. S. Mill *On Liberty*, p. xiv.
19. MCW, XI, p. 313.
20. MCW, XVIII, p. 197.
21. *Gobineau: Selected Political Writings*, ed. M. D. Biddis (London: Cape, 1970), p. 61.
22. H. Maine, *Ancient Law* (London: Dent, 1954), pp. 13–14.
23. W. Bagehot, *Physics and Politics* [1872] (London: Kegan Paul, n.d.), p. 211.
24. C. Darwin, *The Voyage of the Beagle* [1845] (London: Dent, 1955), p. 485. This metaphor may have become something of a cliché for Walter Bagehot quoted with apparent approval the view that: '"There is ... hardly any exaggerating the difference between civilized and uncivilized men; it is greater than the difference between a tame and a wild animal," because man can improve more.' *Physics and Politics*, p. 50.
25. See, for example, Adam Ferguson, *An Essay on the History of Civil Society* [1767] (Cambridge: Cambridge University Press, 1995). See also R. L. Meek, 'The Scottish Contribution to Marxist Sociology', in J. Saville (ed.), *Democracy and the Labour Movement* (London: Lawrence and Wishart, 1954), ch. 3; C. Berry, *Social Theory of the Scottish Enlightenment* (Edinburgh: Edinburgh University Press, 1997).
26. MCW, I, p. 171.
27. Their correspondence has been translated and collected in O. A. Haac (ed.), *The Correspondence of John Stuart Mill and Auguste Comte* (New Brunswick, NJ, 1995). See also J. S. Mill, 'Auguste Comte and Positivism', in MCW, X, pp. 261–368; also published separately (Ann Arbor, MI: University of Michigan Press, 1965).
28. MCW, VIII, p. 912.
29. MCW, X, p. 307.
30. *Marx Engels Selected Works* (London: Lawrence and Wishart, 1962), vol. I, p. 363. The year 1859 was a notable one for the Victorian Charlies, as it also saw the publication of one of Charles Dickens's most political novels, *A Tale of Two Cities*.
31. MCW, XVIII, p. 197.
32. MCW, XXI, p. 87.
33. MCW, X, pp. 205, 233. See also MCW, XVIII, p. 86.
34. MCW, I, p. 173.
35. MCW, X, p. 351.
36. MCW, III, pp. 706–9.
37. MCW, III, p. 756.
38. *On Liberty*, p. 58.

39. See I. Berlin, 'John Stuart Mill and the Ends of Life', in *Four Essays on Liberty* (London: Oxford University Press, 1969). See also J. Plamenatz, *The English Utilitarians* (Oxford: Blackwell, 1958), p. 144.
40. MCW, X, p. 232.
41. Ibid., p. 231.
42. MCW, X, pp. 232, 216.
43. MCW, I, p. 199.
44. G. L. Williams, Introduction to *John Stuart Mill: On Politics and Society* (Hassocks: Harvester Press, 1976), p. 43.
45. MCW, IV, pp. 364, 369, 371.
46. MCW, III, p. 792.
47. Ibid.
48. MCW, II, p. 209.
49. MCW, III, p. 985.
50. MCW, XX, p. 352.
51. MCW, I, p. 239.
52. MCW, X, p. 139.
53. MCW, X, pp. 140–1.
54. MCW, I, p. 9. Any parent of a seven-year-old, such as the present author at the time of first drafting these lines, is bound to be amazed by the achievement.
55. MCW, XXII, p. 253.
56. MCW, I, pp. 336, 338.
57. E. Biagini, 'Liberalism and Direct Democracy: John Stuart Mill and the Model of Ancient Athens', in E. Biagini (ed.), *Citizenship and Community* (Cambridge: Cambridge University Press, 1996), p. 36. Packe, *Mill*, pp. 133–4 attributes 'On Genius' to Harriet's influence.
58. MCW, XI, pp. 273, 324.
59. MCW, XXIV, pp. 1087–8.
60. MCW, XXV, p. 1161.
61. Emphasis added. MCW, XI, pp. 273, 313.

Chapter Five

Civilization Threatened

In the previous chapters barbarism has appeared mainly as a condition of other societies in distant places. For those in the West the term functioned as a means of both denigrating such societies and distancing themselves from them. Trade and imperialism had brought the barbarians into our purview and, hence, they had become objects of both interest and administration. The idea of progress, however, encouraged the sense of a ladder of development that the barbarians might gradually ascend as the civilized West had previously done. Barbarism and civilization, then, were different poles of a developmental process and so became linked on the same continuum. Barbarism is where civilized societies had come from. The point to stress is that even the West itself had once been barbarian. A barbarism that was distant but contemporary now has added to it one that is local but historical.

We thus move from the notion of barbarism and civilization separated by space to the idea of them separated merely by time. This was rather more disturbing, for historical distance seemed closer than geographical distance. To an extent barbarism remained part of Western culture, connected as childhood to adulthood. It was what the West liked to imagine it had risen above and escaped from, yet there still remained a socio-genetic link that could not be undone.

Theories of progress tended to assume an incremental development from savage beginnings through to a presumed rational and peaceful future. Part of the intellectual basis for the emergence of such theories was the earlier notion of a social contract as the transitional moment between a primitive state of nature and a legitimate political order. Thomas Hobbes is known for a lurid description of a state of nature that seems to have been constructed as an inversion of everything that people desired from an ordered society. In his presentation, however, it seemed far from total fantasy, for 'the savage people in many places of America ... live at this day in that brutish manner'.[1] For John Locke the pre-governmental state of nature was everywhere the original condition of mankind. That he had no evidence of our being in that situation was immaterial for "'tis with Commonwealths as with particular Persons, they are commonly ignorant of their own Births and Infancies'. As to the charge that society without government was impossible, Locke produced the evidence of travellers' reports from the Americas.[2] Thus he amalgamated the pre-history of his own society with the then current situation of indigenous Americans.

The point is even more explicit in Rousseau. In his *Discourse on Inequality* he imagined 'when, all setting out from the same point, centuries must have elapsed in the barbarism of the first ages; when the race was already old, and man remained a child'.[3] Clearly here, where '*all*' are 'setting out from the same point', *mankind is one*, and therefore barbarism is part of our history also. Here again we find the idea of a developmental hierarchy, of barbarism as the first stage that eventually leads to civilization and of indigenous American evidence functioning as proof. Clearly the old distinction between barbarism and civilization was being adapted to the idea of progress. No people is ontologically and permanently bracketed with one of the categories. Barbarians are inferior, but they are where all societies started. In Rousseau we also find the idea of man being originally solitary and, as with Mill, sociability and co-operation are seen as the marks of development.

Nearer to Mill's own time, the idea of a sequential connection between barbarism and civilization was familiar from, among others, two authors whose works he knew well. Adam Ferguson believed that '*our* ancestors were in a state of barbarity' and also that the 'inhabitants of Britain, at the time of the first Roman invasions, resembled, in many things, the present natives of North America: they were ignorant of agriculture; they painted their bodies; and used for cloathing, the skins of beasts'.[4] Jeremy Bentham, similarly, saw in the condition of the 'savages of New South Wales' a situation once shared with the 'inhabitants of the part of the globe we call Europe'.[5]

CIVILIZATION AND ITS INSECURITIES

In outlining the role of social contract theory in drawing a link between barbarism and Western civilization, we drew on Hobbes, Locke and Rousseau. For them barbarism was both them and us; currently part of the rest of the world and historically part of Europe. The logic of the social contract method is progressive in that the contract remedies the inconveniences of the state of nature and introduces a legitimate political order. This structure fits easily, though over-schematically, with the developmental sequence from barbarism to civilization and thus with the emerging faith in progress. These thinkers, however, particularly Hobbes and Rousseau, clearly believed that the nature of both man and society rendered all political developments vulnerable to regress. For Hobbes the very nature of man contains 'three principall causes of quarrell. First, Competition; Secondly, Diffidence; Thirdly, Glory.'[6] On this basis the odds would seem to be against the survival of settled and legitimate government. Hobbes, of course, lived at the time of the English Civil War and with him we find a central idea of this study, that civilization is insecure and in danger of relapse. The main function of his state of nature was less to indicate where we had come from than to warn how far we might fall were sovereign power to be undermined. Sheldon Wolin has usefully emphasized that, 'contrary to most later interpreters, Hobbes did not eliminate the state of nature by means of a covenant. *The state of nature is repressed, not transcended.* It exists as a permanent feature of international politics. Domestically it threatens to return every time a law is broken or a promise evaded.'[7]

Hobbes had famously employed the ancient metaphor by which 'that great LEVIATHAN called a COMMONWEALTH, or STATE ... is but an Artificiall Man; though of greater stature and strength than the Naturall, for whose protection and defence it was intended'.[8] One consequence of this usage was drawn explicitly by Rousseau, that the state was as mortal as the individual. Thus the 'body politic, no less than the body of a man, begins to die as soon as it is born, and bears within itself the causes of its own destruction'.[9] This was akin to the vital point, though in less deterministic and hence pessimistic form, that Mill later found in Tocqueville, that ruin can come from within as well as from without.

In addition to the pessimistic conclusions that could be drawn from the nature of man and, by analogy, that of society, was the evidence of actual human history. To the educated classes, to which Mill *par excellence* belonged, the fate of earlier great civilizations was not encouraging. Almost a century before *On Liberty*, Rousseau had written a chapter on 'The Death of the Body Politic'. It commenced with a melancholy warning: 'Such is the natural and inevitable inclination of the best constituted governments. If Sparta and Rome perished, what state can hope to last for ever?'[10]

Soon after Rousseau, Edward Gibbon's *Decline and Fall of the Roman Empire* (1776–88) suggested that an important sign of imperial decay was that the 'minds of men were gradually reduced to the same level, the fire of genius was extinguished'.[11] This is exactly the fear that Mill was to express, and John Burrow has interestingly linked Mill's description of mass society with 'the characteristics of Gibbon's corrupted Romans', noting, furthermore, that there is 'a good deal in Mill's writings ... consonant with long-standing Whig ideas and concerns ... Mill's historical anxiety and even pessimism forms a common background ... There is the same anxiety for liberty and the same sense that current social changes place it in jeopardy.'[12] The historians knew, of course, that the ancient empires had emerged, grown, flourished and eventually decayed. For David Hume it was the task of the historian 'to

remark the rise, progress, declension and final extinction of the most flourishing empires; the virtues, which contributed to their greatness, and the vices
which drew on their ruin'.[13] Simultaneously with Gibbon, Adam Ferguson had
written on *The History of the Progress and Termination of the Roman
Republic* (1783), expanding on some of the points he had made in 'Of the
Decline of Nations', the penultimate part of his *Essay on the History of Civil
Society* (1767). In his attacks on Warren Hastings, Edmund Burke drew on a
long-standing fear that empires abroad can lead to destruction at home. Iain
Hampsher-Monk has reminded us that

> classical scholars of politics and their renaissance followers agreed that the
> acquisition of empire – as the examples of Athens and Rome showed – was
> bound to bring about the eventual destruction of the free institutions which had
> given rise to it, and their substitution by a single absolute ruler. This was the
> inevitable consequence of the corruption of the society's original manners and
> virtue through dependence on standing armies, and by the influx of wealth, alien
> morals and exotic customs that resulted from empire.[14]

All this, one might think, was before Mill's time, yet the rising popularity,
from the late eighteenth century onwards, of theories of progress had not
exorcized the spectre of decline.[15] From Mill's acquaintances one can
construct a catalogue of pessimistic prognoses. To start within the family, his
father had been upset by a speech on parliamentary reform from Thomas
Atwood, founder of the Birmingham Political Union and a later Chartist. His
opinions, thought James Mill, 'if they were to spread, would be the subver-
sion of civilized society; worse than the overwhelming deluge of Huns and
Tartars'.[16] Here, quite explicitly, the internal threat is greater than any from
outside.

From James Mill we may turn to his friend and mentor Jeremy Bentham,
for whom society was actually insufficiently modern and contained within it
dangerous remnants of savagery. Bentham wrote *The Theory of Legislation*
during the period of the Napoleonic Wars, and noted that during warfare
'civilized society returns almost to the savage state'. In command of this
development was the aristocracy. On this basis Bentham was happy to invert
their conventional status, for they presented, he argued, the worst rather than,
as they supposed, the best aspect of our culture. They were powerful and
undesirable remnants of a less civilized age.

> Thus we see, in ages of barbarism, that the upper classes have divided their
> whole life between war; the chase, which is the image of war; the animal
> functions; and long repasts, of which drunkenness was the greatest attraction.
> Such is the whole history of a great proprietor, a great feudal lord of the Middle
> Ages. The privilege of this noble warrior, or of this noble hunter, extended into

83

the midst of a more civilized society the occupations and the character of a savage.[17]

A further intimation of national decline that Mill knew well was in Macaulay's merciless attack on James Mill in the *Edinburgh Review* article of 1829. Macaulay believed that the 'civilized part of the world has now nothing to fear from the hostility of savage nations'. Instead the danger was from within. 'But is it possible', he asked, 'that in the bosom of civilization itself may be engendered the malady which shall destroy it?' Here Macaulay envisaged not merely stagnation but actual regress. 'Is it possible', he continued, 'that, in two or three hundred years, a few lean and half-naked fishermen may divide with owls and foxes the ruins of the greatest European cities – may wash their nets amidst the relics of her gigantic docks, and build their huts out of the capitals of her stately cathedrals?'[18] In his *Autobiography*, John Stuart Mill conceded that though the tone of Macaulay's article was not to his liking, there were many points that had caused him to rethink his own position.[19]

Mill and Thomas Carlyle had been close friends during the 1830s, but in time Mill became increasingly displeased with Carlyle's intolerant and reactionary opinions. Mill had lent Carlyle some of the material used for the latter's *The French Revolution* and had greatly praised it in the *London and Westminster Review* of July 1837. Here Mill would have noted the stock conservative motif of a dubious human nature threatening to undermine centuries of achievement. 'Alas then,' asked Carlyle, 'is man's civilisation only a wrappage, through which the savage nature of him can still burst, infernal as ever? Nature still makes him; and has an Infernal in her as well as a Celestial.'[20]

With Hobbes and Carlyle we find the conservative theme that civilization is fragile and that strong government is necessary to control the savagery lurking just below the surface. On this notion a society could complete a cyclical journey from barbarism to civilization and back again. This, we shall find, was not actually Mill's position. What he feared was rather a stalling of civilization through the very forces it had itself produced; a dialectic of civilization within civilization. This would involve a loss of Western global leadership through standing still while others were advancing. Mill, then, did not occupy the bleakest point on the spectrum of contemporary pessimism, though he shared some of the prevailing insecurities.

Though human nature might have its dark side; and though it was ominous that previous civilizations had eventually declined, the great success story of mid-nineteenth-century Britain was its astonishing economic output. One small island on the fringes of its continent had achieved an unparalleled domination of world trade. That surely was cause for celebration and the 1851 Great Exhibition was a successful attempt to provide it. And yet British self-confidence was not unalloyed. Rapid advance seemed to have produced its own insecurities. To some observers the first industrial nation seemed out on its own, and possibly out of control in uncharted waters and with little idea of where it was so rapidly heading. Seymour Drescher has noted that Alexis de Tocqueville 'like many French observers ... looked on the rapid industrialization of England as a gigantic and dangerous gamble'. It seemed that the 'English people had simply been carried away by the passion for wealth'.[21] For all his supposed identification with both liberalism and political economy, Mill was quite critical of the commercial spirit and sympathetic with the fairly common view that material advance seemed to have been gained at the cost of both ethical values and social solidarity.

Furthermore, British pre-eminence was partially based upon economic progress, but even this was not guaranteed. Remarkable inventions and the establishment of the factory system had facilitated mass production and, consequently, the possibility of unprecedented output, but none of this could guarantee stable or increasing levels of actual demand. Recurrent booms and slumps threw the workers into dangerous bouts of extreme poverty and the employers into bankruptcy. The most vivid image of this was Marx's comparison of modern society with Goethe's sorcerer's apprentice, 'no longer able to control the powers of the nether world whom he has called up by his spells'.[22] Mill, it seems, had never heard of Marx, but even from the foremost advocates of political economy, writers with whose works Mill had been brought up, one of whom, David Ricardo, was his father's closest friend[23] and the 'high priest of the Utilitarian economic doctrine',[24] he found reasons for disquiet.

We must be careful to get the balance right here. Political economy from Smith to Mill had its optimistic aspects. It was an attempt at a unified social science that outlined the pattern of progression from hunting, pastoral and farming societies through to modern commercial society. It recorded, then, a story of outstanding success in raising human productivity. Where it fits into our theme is in its profound uncertainty that current commercial achievements could be maintained or that the wealth generated could raise the situation of the mass of the labouring population. In *The Wealth of Nations* Adam Smith had outlined how the workers' wages sank down to the level where they were only just sufficient for survival. A man 'whose whole life is spent in performing a few simple operations ... generally becomes as stupid and ignorant as it is possible for a human creature to become ... But in every improved and civilised society, this is the state into which the labouring poor, the great body of the people, must necessarily fall.'[25] That in 'every improved and civilised society' the mass of those who perform the basic productive work are kept poor, stupid and only just alive seems not to be a satisfactory outcome of human development, let alone the greatest happiness of the greatest number. It was not merely that wages tended to decline; profits would also, and the real wealth of the society would become stationary. Smith believed that this tendency could be temporarily stemmed by new investment opportunities or expansion into new territories, but nevertheless, on its own reasoning, political economy could not avoid a forecast of decline.

Ricardo, following Malthus, had emphasized the deleterious consequences of increasing populations. In order to feed more people less fertile land had to be taken into cultivation. Thus the same amount of labour and capital brought in less produce and so wages would fall to subsistence level. This would lead to a 'stationary and melancholic state' from which only the landlord would benefit. This was precisely the class that John Stuart Mill liked least. Ricardo foresaw, then, a fall of both wages and profits leading to prolonged economic crises.

So, to summarize, the view that the economy was unstable was found even in the writings of the political economists who were the foremost advocates of the system. From Adam Smith, Malthus, Ricardo, Nassau Senior and even, in some respects, from his own father, Mill learnt of the inevitability of population outstripping production, of the wages of labour necessarily falling to subsistence level, of the chronic passage of the trade cycle from glut to unemployment, of the long-term tendency for profits and wages to fall and of the likelihood that society would stagnate. This, then, was what Mill had learnt of the impact of the economy on society. Even more important for the argument outlined in *On Liberty* was what he learnt of the changing impact of society on the individual.

THE RISE OF MASS SOCIETY

We shall shortly consider the extent to which Mill followed Tocqueville in attributing to modernity the rise of mass society and the consequent threat to the freedom of the individual. Tocqueville's was, of course, a distinctly aristocratic account in that the pre-modern social order was held to be more conducive to freedom than its successor. One of Tocqueville's predecessors as a theorist of social conformity was Jean-Jacques Rousseau. His direct influence on Mill was minimal, but he is worth mentioning in that the key themes that concern us are so clearly prefigured in his writings. In striking contrast to Tocqueville, Rousseau saw social conformity as already prevalent in the aristocratic *ancien régime*. This certainly does not refute Tocqueville's notion that conformity correlates with development, but with Rousseau the relevant development was that of civilization and its creation of new needs. Rousseau was opposed to the increasing division of labour. For him a free person was one who could meet his own needs, and, on this basis, the freest people were the peasantry, for their requirements were few and they could, on the whole, provide for themselves. Elsewhere 'the increase of artificial wants only binds so many more chains upon the people'. Those who become dependent on others, then, have to adapt to their tastes and manners. They become what would later be called 'other-oriented', and, as the following would seem to imply, precise adjustment of behaviour is particularly required for those in contact with what is called good society.

> In our day, now that more subtle study and a more refined taste have reduced the art of pleasing to a system, there prevails in modern manners a servile and deceptive conformity; so that one would think every mind had been cast in the same mould. Politeness requires this thing; decorum that; ceremony has its forms, and fashion its laws, and these we must always follow, never the promptings of our own nature.
>
> We no longer dare seem what we really are, but lie under a perpetual restraint; in the meantime the herd of men, which we call society, all act under the same circumstances exactly alike, unless very particular and powerful motives prevent them.[26]

We have introduced Rousseau to suggest that social conformity pre-dates the mass society feared by Tocqueville and Mill. What mass society did was to alter the direction of social pressures. As Mill made clear in the first chapter of *On Liberty*, tyranny was traditionally seen as a misuse of power by the monarch, but in the democratic age the threat to freedom came from below, from society itself. Society, then, was suddenly both powerful and dangerous. According to a prestigious line of thought, stretching back to the very origins of Western thought, democracy was associated with irrationality, instability, insecurity of property and a mob rule that eventually ended in tyranny and the decline of civilization. Modern versions of this refrain had been provided in Burke and de Maistre's reactions to the French Revolution.

Here, then, we have one notion of mass society. It indicates the direct intrusion of a violent mob on to the political stage. This was the way in which Mill's generation feared the mass, as we can see from Carlyle's *The French Revolution* and Dickens's *Barnaby Rudge* and *A Tale of Two Cities*. Carlyle's notion of democracy and mass society was based on the French experience, in which a traditional aristocratic system had been violently destroyed. From Tocqueville, however, Mill learnt of a quite different model of mass society, the American one. Here the mass had no aristocrats to string up on lamp-posts; there was little violence and no guillotine. In the United States mass society was emerging from a settled constitutional order based on representative government.

Alexis de Tocqueville was in the United States for less than one year, from May 1831 to February 1832. The ostensible purpose of his journey was to visit American penal institutions, though his basic intention was to study democracy in its most developed form. His two volumes on *Democracy in America* were published in 1835 and 1840. As a result of their success Tocqueville became an instant celebrity and, ever since, the books have been taken as the classic work on the United States by a foreigner.

87

For Tocqueville democracy constituted less a political system than a social condition in which the differences between the classes were constantly diminishing. Democracy was the opposite of aristocracy. It signified the replacement of class difference by a mass society in which 'the tyranny of the majority' threatened all those who thought differently.

The first aspect of mass society had been the violent physical intrusion of the lower orders on to the political stage. This had happened in France and less dramatically in America. On Tocqueville's logic the French Revolution cannot have been the cause of democracy, though it might have accelerated it, for the tendency had been evident for the previous 700 years and was determined by providence.

The mass society that Tocqueville found in the United States was based on a society where class differentials were disappearing. There were fewer obstacles to this process than in Europe, where aristocracy was solidly entrenched. In Tocqueville's first volume American democracy appeared happily, and fortuitously, decentralized although democracy in the abstract was said to have the opposite tendency. By Volume Two, Tocqueville was less optimistic and also less focused solely on the United States. His subject increasingly became that of democracy in general, and the basic tendency towards centralization, if not despotism, was one from which even the United States no longer seemed immune.

Under democracy, according to Tocqueville, traditional authority and deference suffer a decline. At first the democratization of values led individuals to place intellectual authority in themselves, but in time they came to feel too isolated, weak and insecure against the mass, and so their own self-confidence and self-reliance were gradually replaced by a condition of 'almost unbounded confidence in the judgement of the public'. The tendency was one in which particular authorities come to be replaced by the unlimited authority of the generality. No laws were needed to produce this effect, for public disapproval was enough. Against it there is no alternative and no appeal. So arose 'a new physiognomy of servitude' in which public opinion became 'a species of religion, and the majority its ministering prophet'. Variety, thought Tocqueville, was 'disappearing from the human race; the same ways of acting, thinking, and feeling are to be met with all over the world'.[27] In Europe, as in America, secondary powers, or what he also called 'intermediate institutions', were losing their efficacy. The privileges of the old nobility and the powers of individual cities and other provincial authorities were gradually being destroyed. An omnipotent sameness was replacing them. From this situation Tocqueville envisaged a supreme power which

> covers the surface of society with a network of small, complicated rules, minute and uniform, through which the most original minds and the most energetic

characters cannot penetrate, to rise above the crowd. The will of man is not shattered, but softened, bent, and guided; men are seldom forced by it to act, but they are constantly restrained from acting. Such a power does not destroy, but it prevents existence; it does not tyrannize, but it compresses, enervates, extinguishes, and stupefies a people, till each nation is reduced to nothing better than a flock of timid and industrious animals, of which the government is the shepherd.[28]

We see, then, that the mass that Tocqueville found in America was not like that of France. It was not an active mass but a passive one; not one that rouses but one that suppresses. It induces torpor rather than violence, submission rather than heroism and conformity rather than eccentricity. It subdues rather than activates, but under its influence liberty is as endangered as under any explicit dictatorship. Tocqueville's terminology might well have gained currency through his readers' fears of an aroused modern mass, but we see that his analysis was of a different sort. His mass derived its power not from political action but from its sociological characteristic, that, due to its numerical preponderance, it had no serious rival. For Tocqueville, absence of class differentials produced absence of diversity as for the first time the same social norms and values came to dominate the whole society.

Mill wrote long reviews of both Tocqueville's volumes and was instrumental in introducing his ideas to an English readership. He wrote on Volume One of *Democracy in America* in the *London Review* of October 1835. His account is particularly interesting for our purposes, both for his first comments on Tocqueville and also because Mill's remarks on mass society contrast so strikingly with his views in *On Liberty* nearly a quarter of a century later. Though the most graphic warnings concerning mass society had to await Tocqueville's second volume, the first volume contained a particularly pertinent chapter on the 'Unlimited Power of the Majority in the United States, and Its Consequences'. Even though the following chapter is on the 'Causes Which Mitigate the Tyranny of the Majority in the United States', there is certainly enough in Volume One to warn of mass society and how its dangers were structurally linked to the democratic condition.

In the review Mill noted Tocqueville's description of 'a tyranny exercised over opinions, more than over persons, which he is apprehensive of. He dreads lest all individuality of character, and independence of thought and sentiment, should be prostrated under the despotic yoke of public opinion.'[29] Tocqueville, of course, looked to America for the future towards which other civilized countries were moving. The United States provided a singular example of a wider development. Mill, however, given though he was to the notion of social development, did not view it in such a constricted and generalized manner. He was confident that Britain had its own particular safeguards and though he was otherwise no friend of 'endowed institutions for education' (often instruments of religious dogmatism), nor of the aristocracy (enjoying unearned benefits and privileges), he now saw in both 'a security, far greater than has ever existed in America, against the tyranny of public opinion over the individual mind'. He believed that a leisured class would always both enjoy and encourage individual thought and also maintain a level of cultivation that would serve as a standard for others. Mill was confident that this class would provide a 'salutary corrective of all the inconveniences to which democracy is liable. We cannot, under any modification of the laws of England, look forward to a period when this grand security for the progressiveness of the human species will not exist.' Furthermore, Mill was certain that democracy's negative tendencies could be overcome if the 'superior spirits' put themselves to the 'instruction of the democracy' rather than to 'the patching of the old worn-out machinery of aristocracy'.[30]

Who, then, constitutes this leisured class to which Mill granted such significance? In that Mill first referred to the actual existence of a class possessing 'hereditary leisure' we can only assume he meant the landed aristocracy. He then, however, seemed to elide the existence of a hereditary leisured aristocracy with a secular version of Coleridge's clerisy – an intellectual elite that sets standards of both individuality and 'mental cultivation'. This syncretism is the more astonishing in view of Mill's simultaneous rejection of the 'worn-out machinery of aristocracy' and also of his otherwise consistent opposition to aristocratic power, wealth and principles.

Mill's review of Tocqueville's second volume appeared, like the book itself, in 1840. At the level of general appraisal, Mill's comments were overwhelmingly positive. Tocqueville, said Mill, had produced 'the first philosophical book ever written on Democracy, as it manifests itself in modern society'. It marked the 'beginning of a new era in the scientific study of politics'. One of Tocqueville's phrases, that of 'the tyranny of the majority' had, said Mill, been adopted by Sir Robert Peel, and had, consequently, led to the view among 'country gentlemen that M. de Tocqueville is one of the pillars of Conservatism'.[31] This was an error, but a happy one, for it had led to the work becoming known to a British readership. However, the British country gentlemen, like their French counterparts, might have been less than happy to learn that providence had ordained aristocratic decline. Whatever their future, Mill was quite certain that providence would have nothing to do with it. Possibly for reasons of tact and prudence he totally disregarded the important theological basis of Tocqueville's argument.

Mill also implicitly rejected the construction of a general process from evidence drawn only from France and the United States. It was in France that Tocqueville had observed the long-term trend of aristocratic decline. Mill, surveying British history, saw things rather differently. In place of disappearance he saw mere deterioration. The British aristocracy seemed no longer capable of taking the lead in any significant area of national life. Mill, however, did not expect its redundancy to lead to extinction. In fact, if only it would rise to the challenge, it still had a task to perform: that of strengthening diversity in a society where public opinion was becoming 'more and more the supreme power'.[32]

Mill, then, looking at Great Britain, found no confirmation of Tocqueville's rather fatalistic general theory. Here there had been no revolution, as in France, and no passion for equality, as in the United States. Very much to 'the contrary, all ranks seem to have a passion for inequality'. If, for Tocqueville, equality was the basis of mass society and mental conformity, then England ought to have been safe. This was not the case, however. For Mill social conformity could have other causes, not just the disappearance of class differentials but also the rise of commercial society and the over-preponderance of one particular class. Mill noted a change in the balance of social power in Britain. The influence of the upper classes seemed to be 'diminishing; while that of the middle and even the lower classes is increasing, and likely to increase'.[33] We find here a significantly lower estimate of England than in the previous review. It would, said Mill,

be difficult to show any country in which ... the growing insignificance of individuals in comparison with the mass ... is more marked and conspicuous than in England ... No rank in society is now exempt from the fear of being peculiar, the unwillingness to be, or to be thought, in any respect, original. Hardly any thing now depends upon individuals, but all upon classes, and among classes mainly upon the middle class. That class is now the power in society, the arbiter of fortune and success.

So, to emphasize the point, Mill was grateful to Tocqueville for highlighting the causes of mass society, but, in striking contrast, did not see equality as its necessary social basis. Even without equality, newspapers and the railways were playing their part in reducing local particularities and creating a more homogeneous society. The aristocracy, if they were to be any use at all, might still render some social service as a countervailing power. This, regrettably, they seemed unable to do, for the 'daily actions of every peer and peeress are falling more and more under the yoke of *bourgeois* opinion'.[34] In contrast to his 1835 review, Mill now disaggregated the leisured from the learned class and hoped that both would provide 'a great support for opinions and sentiments different from those of the mass'. To them he added the agricultural class, for their 'natural tendencies' were 'in many respects the reverse of those of a manufacturing and commercial' class.[35] In modern society, however, the ascendancy of the latter was inevitable, but 'under due limitations, ought not to be regarded as an evil ... Now, as ever, the great problem in government is to prevent the strongest from becoming the only power.'[36] So, to conclude, in the review of Tocqueville's second volume Mill argued that there was a mass society problem in Britain; it stemmed, however, from different causes than those outlined by Tocqueville; a social base existed for resistance to its tendencies; but it was still unclear whether the relevant groups would do the job that Mill hoped from them.

NOTES

1. T. Hobbes, *Leviathan* [1651] (London: Dent, 1962), p. 65.
2. J. Locke, *Two Treatises of Government*, introduction P. Laslett [1690] (New York: Mentor, 1965), second treatise, para. 101. See ibid., para. 102 and Introduction pp. 149–61, which lists the books known to have been in Locke's library.
3. J. J. Rousseau, *The Social Contract. Discourses*, ed. G. D. H. Cole (London: Dent, 1961), p. 188.
4. Emphasis added. A Ferguson, *An Essay on the History of Civil Society* [1767] (Cambridge: Cambridge University Press, 1995), pp. 77, 75. See also pp. 78, 114.
5. B. Parekh (ed.), *Bentham's Political Thought* (London: Croom Helm, 1973) p. 269.
6. Hobbes, *Leviathan*, p. 64.
7. Emphasis added. S. S. Wolin, 'Democracy and the Welfare State: The Political and Theoretical Connections Between Staatsräson and Wohlfahrtsstaatsräson', *Political Theory*, 15 (4), 1987, p. 484.
8. Hobbes, *Leviathan*, p. 1.
9. J. J. Rousseau, *Social Contract*, trans. and intro. by M. Cranston (Harmondsworth: Penguin Books, 1968), p. 134.
10. Ibid.
11. Quoted in J. Burrow, *Whigs and Liberals: Continuity and Change in English Political Thought* (Oxford: Clarendon, 1988), p. 121.
12. Burrow, *Whigs and Liberals*, pp. 85, 102, 104; see also pp. 115–17, 121.
13. Quoted in R. Porter, *Enlightenment: Britain and the Creation of the Modern World* (Harmondsworth: Penguin Books, 2001), p. 232.
14. I. Hampsher-Monk, *The Political Philosophy of Edmund Burke* (London: Longman, 1987) , p. 15
15. See W. E. Houghton, *The Victorian Frame of Mind, 1830–1870* (New Haven, CT: Yale University Press, 1985), ch. 3, 'Anxiety'. For a similar mood in Germany, see Ludwig Uhland's remarkable poem 'Des Sängers Fluch', in K. Breul, *The Romantic Movement in German Literature* (Cambridge: Heffer, 1927), pp. 297–9 and F. von Schlegel, *The Philosophy of History* [1828] (London: Bohn, 1846), pp. 92–3.
16. Quoted in Packe, *Mill*, p. 101.
17. J. Bentham, *The Theory of Legislation* [1802] (London: Kegan Paul, 1931), pp. 109, 376.
18. *James Mill: Political Writings*, ed. T. Ball (Cambridge: Cambridge University Press, 1992), p. 297.
19. See MCW, I, pp. 165–9.
20. T. Carlyle, *The French Revolution: A History* (London: Chapman and Hall, 1891), Part III, p. 317.

21. S. Drescher, *Dilemmas of Democracy: Tocqueville and Modernization* (Pittsburgh, PA: University of Pittsburgh Press, 1968), p. 68.

22. *Marx Engels Collected Works*, vol. 6 (London: Lawrence and Wishart, 1976), p. 489.

23. According to Packe, *Mill*, p. 38.

24. E. Stokes, *The English Utilitarians and India* (Delhi: Oxford University Press, 1992), p. 88.

25. Quoted in A. Walker, *Marx: His Theory and Its Context* (London: Longman, 1978), pp. 156–7.

26. J. J. Rousseau, 'Arts and Sciences', in *The Social Contract: Discourses*, pp. 121, 122. 'It will not be possible to understand Rousseau and his influence ... unless he is seen as expressing a reaction to court rationality and to the suppression of "feeling" in court life.' N. Elias, *The Court Society* (New York: Pantheon Books, 1983), p. 113.

27. A. de Toqueville, *Democracy in America*, 2 vols (New York: Vintage Books, 1945), vol. 2, pp. 11, 12, 13, 240.

28. Ibid., p. 337.

29. MCW, XVIII, p. 81.

30. Ibid., pp. 85–6.

31. Ibid., p. 156.

32. Ibid., p. 162.

33. Ibid., p. 163.

34. Ibid., p. 194.

35. Ibid., p. 198.

36. Ibid., p. 200.

Chapter Six

Standstill: The Case of China

In Chapter 3 we dealt at some length with both Mills' views of India. For the younger Mill India was backward and barbarian. China, however, was in a very different category. Here a once advanced civilization had stagnated from within, brought to a standstill by its own internal forces. In *On Liberty* Mill used this example to show that even a great and developed civilization could come to a halt and so lose its global pre-eminence. Its particular situation was, therefore, relevant to the West in a way that India's wasn't.

WESTERN VIEWS OF CHINA

Alongside the gradual European discovery and exploitation of much of the rest of the world there emerged the process of evaluative comparison. In the Americas it seemed that man in the original state of nature could still be found. In the East more complex societies existed with large cities, extensive trading connections and ingenious religious mythologies. Mill's comments on both India and China form, of course, part of a far wider Western discourse on the East.[1] For him these two countries were in fundamentally different categories. For others the East was one, India and China being merely separate examples of the same general stagnation. Montesquieu, for example, saw in 'the peoples of the East ... a certain laziness of the spirit, naturally bound with that of the body, which makes that spirit incapable of any action, any effort, any application'. Such peoples were consequently so inflexible that any 'laws, mores, and manners, even those that seem not to matter, like the fashion in clothing, remain in the East today as they were a thousand years ago'.[2] From the *Edinburgh Review*, to which both Mills also contributed, an anonymous author noted that the 'spirit of Oriental institutions was unfriendly to the vigorous expansion of thought. In all ages of the world, Asia has been deprived of the light of freedom, and has in consequence incurred the doom of absolute sterility in the higher fruits of moral and mental culture'.[3] In Germany Mill's contemporary Leopold von Ranke (1795–1886) referred to

Eastern civilizations as 'nations of eternal standstill'.[4] Walter Bagehot, a critic of Mill's views on the emancipation of women, showed in 1872 that, like Mill, he was concerned to ascertain the placing of Asian societies. He noted that the 'great difficulty which history records is not that of the first step, but that of the second step'. This was where Asian societies – 'the whole family of arrested civilisations' – were placed. They seemed 'to be ready to advance to something good – to have prepared all the means to advance to something good – and then to have stopped, and not advanced. India, Japan, China, almost every sort of Oriental civilisation, though differing in nearly all other things, are in this alike.'[5]

In 1797 Charles Grant had used much the same analysis of India that Mill was to apply to China. Grant was one of the main Evangelicals hoping to Christianize India. In a work that was republished as a Parliamentary Paper in 1813 and also in 1832, and so might have come to Mill's attention, Grant argued that India was a civilization that had stagnated. He recommended 'the further civilization of a people, who had very early made a considerable progress in improvement, but who, by deliberate and successful plans of fraud and imposition, were rendered first stationary, then retrograde'.[6] Given the nature of Mill's employment, it is certain that India would have been more on his mind than China was. It is, therefore, worth explaining why he did not follow Grant in using India as his warning example of how a society could stagnate. The difference between them is that Grant acknowledged that India had already become a civilization, whereas Mill did not. For Mill China could serve as a warning to the West precisely because it had previously advanced before relapsing into standstill. As we saw in Chapter 3, India was seen in a quite different light as a society that had not even advanced in the first place.[7]

J. J. Clarke notes that François Quesnay (1694–1744) *like so many of his contemporaries*, regarded China as an ideal society that provided a model for Europe to follow'.[8] In the eighteenth century Voltaire was the most prominent Western admirer of China. In comparing the sentiments of ancient peoples he concluded that the mandarins of China were alone in their freedom from superstition. He used China as Montesquieu used Persia: as a stick with which to beat the *ancien régime* for its irrationality and intolerance. The emperor, said Voltaire, might be an autocrat but he was 'both the first philosopher and the first preacher of the empire; his edicts are almost always both informative and morally wise'.[9] It is certain that Voltaire would not have made a similar compliment to his own monarch.

This approach did not last. Among Voltaire's younger French contemporaries Rousseau regarded China as a decadent civilization and Condorcet saw it as in a state of 'shameful stagnation'. The people had 'preceded all others in the arts and sciences, only to see themselves successively eclipsed by them all'. Even the invention of printing, which in Condorcet's general theory of civilization was the eighth of ten stages, had failed to produce progress in

China.[10] From Germany Herder viewed China 'as an old ruin on the verge of the World'. It had the 'internal circulation of a dormouse in its winter sleep'.[11] In England, Bentham's *Book of Fallacies* commenced with what he called 'The Wisdom of Our Ancestors: or Chinese Argument'.[12]

In an age of spectacular European development and transformation a society that was both enormously large and apparently stationary by deliberate policy was a source of both amazement and disapproval. China, says one historian, 'was becoming for the West at large the archetype of obstructive conservatism'.[13] Even prior to the influence of Tocqueville, Mill's voluminous reading would have acquainted him with the conventional stereotypes. From David Hume he might have learnt that 'China is one vast empire ... The authority of any teacher, such as Confucius, was propagated easily from one corner of the empire to the other. None had the courage to resist the torrent of popular opinion.'[14] Mill was also well acquainted with and an admirer of the writings of Adam Smith and Thomas Malthus. In *The Wealth of Nations* Smith had noted that 'China has long been one of the richest, that is, one of the most fertile, best cultivated, most industrious, and most populous countries in the world. It seems, however, to have long been stationary.'[15] Malthus concurred that 'it is generally allowed that the wealth of China has long been stationary'.[16] James Mill touched on China in a piece for the *Edinburgh Review* of July 1809. John Stuart was three at the time and, even with his remarkable development, we shall not assume that he read it on publication. He could well have been acquainted with his father's views on the subject, however. For James Mill China had not developed and then ossified. It hadn't even made a start. The Chinese were categorized 'in the infancy, or very little advanced beyond the infancy, of fixed, or agricultural society'. From the standpoint of utilitarianism their placing on the felicific calculus was low. 'It is not possible for a people' to be 'less favourable to happiness, than the Chinese are. Their government is a despotism in the very simplest and rudest form.' There was not, James Mill assumed, 'one of the arts in China in a state which indicates a stage of civilization beyond the infancy of agricultural society'.[17]

Hegel was certainly not one of Mill's main sources, but we can mention his own distinctive presentation of the Western attitude towards the East:

> Early do we see China advancing to the condition in which it is found at this day; for as the contrast between objective existence and subjective freedom of movement in it, is still wanting, every change is excluded, and the fixedness of a character which recurs perpetually, takes the place of what we should call the truly historical. China and India lie, as it were, still outside the World's History, as the mere presupposition of elements whose combination must be waited for to constitute their vital progress.

Africa, in contrast, 'is no historical part of the World; it has no movement or development to exhibit'.[18] China and India were at least part of the process of development – at the beginning. Africa was not even that. The contrast is illuminating, for it later came to form the essence of Mill's threat. An uncivilized country provides no danger or warning to a civilized one. On the other hand, a civilized country that has ossified forewarns of the most terrible fate possible for a proud and advanced country.

Just around the years when *On Liberty* was being written and published Friedrich Engels wrote of China as 'the rotting semi-civilisation of the oldest state in the world'.[19] Marx described China as 'vegetating in the teeth of time' and as 'that living fossil', noting that 'the Oriental empires demonstrate constant immobility in their social structure'.[20] Marx and Engels were much more aware than Mill that commerce was ending Chinese isolation and stationariness. Mill keeps to the old cliché. Yet, as we shall soon discuss, just as Mill was writing *On Liberty*, British gunboats were forcing China into contact with the Western world.

For the nearest proximity to Mill's view, however, we must return to the French, to Constant and Tocqueville. In 1813 Benjamin Constant wrote a work highly pertinent to this stage of our enquiry: *The Spirit of Conquest and Usurpation and Their Relation to European Civilization*. It contains a chapter on a theme that would later be central to Mill: 'The Effects of Arbitrary Power upon Intellectual Progress.' Here Constant explained that 'the lethargy of a nation in which there is no public opinion spreads to its government, whatever it does. Having failed to keep the nation awake, it ends by falling asleep with it. Thus in a nation in which thought is enslaved, everything is silent, every-thing sinks, everything degenerates and is degraded.' As evidence Constant turned to the histories of ancient Egypt and Greece. In a footnote he also included China. 'The government of that country has succeeded in enslaving thought and reducing it to a mere instrument ... No-one dares to open a new course, or to stray in any way from prescribed opinions.' This was history from which a lesson could be learnt for, in anticipation of Tocqueville and Mill, Constant warned that his own country could suffer the same fate. In a clear dissociation from Napoleonic triumphs, Constant concluded that this 'history will be that of France, of this country privileged by nature and by chance, if despotism perseveres in the silent oppression which it has for a long time disguised under the vain brilliance of external triumphs'.[21]

For Constant modern despotism threatened to produce stagnation. We move nearer to Mill with Tocqueville's warning that the same fate could also result from modern democracy. As we shall see, the threat of Western stagna-tion comes when it has produced a mass society, and the most influential warning Mill received on this danger was from Tocqueville. Tocqueville's second volume of *Democracy in America* begins with twenty-one chapters under the general heading of 'Influence of Democracy on the Action of

Intellect in the United States'. His findings form a catalogue of failures. In the very first sentence we read 'that in no country in the civilized world is less attention paid to philosophy than in the United States'. Later we learn that the 'inhabitants of the United States have, then, at present, properly speaking, no literature' and also 'no poets'. In 'few of the civilized nations of our time have the higher sciences made less progress than in the United States'. To someone of Mill's commitment to education this must have been a dire prognosis of democracy's tendency. It was in this context that Tocqueville used China as a warning of how freedom could be lost. China, indeed, provided the most necessary warning because it was the one for which Europe was unprepared. 'Because', wrote Tocqueville, 'the civilization of ancient Rome perished in consequence of the invasion of the Barbarians, we are perhaps too apt to think that civilization cannot perish in any other manner.' In China addiction to practical science had overcome concern with theory. 'The Chinese, in follow-ing the track of their forefathers, had forgotten the reasons by which the latter had been guided', which is exactly the point that Mill made about religion in *On Liberty*. 'They still', said Tocqueville,

> used the formula without asking for its meaning; they retained the instrument, but they no longer possessed the art of altering or renewing it. *The Chinese then, had lost the power of change; for them all improvement was impossible*. They were compelled at all times and in all points to imitate their predecessors lest they should stray into utter darkness by deviating for an instant from the path already laid down for them. The source of human knowledge was all but dry; and though the stream still ran on, it could neither swell its waters nor alter its course (emphasis added).

The point we are meant to take from this comes in the final sentence of the chapter. Civilizations can fall not only from without but also from within. 'It is then a fallacy to flatter ourselves with the reflection that the barbarians are still far from us; for if there are some nations that allow civilization to be torn from their grasp, there are others who themselves trample it underfoot.'[22]

In 1840, the year that Mill read and reviewed Tocqueville's second volume, he wrote to him to confirm their common outlook:

> Among so many ideas which are *more or less new to me* I have found (what I consider a very great compliment to the justness of my own views) that one of your great general conclusions is exactly that which I have been almost alone in standing up for here, and have not as far as I know made a single disciple – namely that the real danger in democracy, the real evil to be struggled against, and which all human resources employed while it is not yet too late are not more than sufficient to fence off – is not anarchy or love of change, but Chinese stagnation & immobility.[23]

This passage is of interest to us for a number of reasons. It is not quite Mill's first delineation of China as a warning to the West. That had come two years earlier in his essay on 'Bentham'. There Mill had written that all progressive countries had derived their greatness from 'an organised opposition to the ruling power ... Wherever some such quarrel has not been going on ... society has either hardened into Chinese stationariness, or fallen into dissolution'. Where there is no opposition, 'there the human race will inevitably degenerate; and the question, whether the United States, for instance, will in time sink into another China (also a most commercial and industrious nation) resolves itself ... into the question, whether such a centre of resistance will gradually evolve itself or not'.[24] In the 'Bentham' essay the China imagery cannot have come from Tocqueville, nor can the crucial warning of the Chinese example as a negative warning for the United States, as the essay pre-dates Tocqueville's second volume by two years. In terms of influence the letter to Tocqueville is rather vague, particularly in its reference to ideas that are 'more or less new to me', but yet constitutes a 'compliment to the justness of my own views'. Presumably, then, the novelty was 'less' rather than 'more'. Furthermore, Mill was concurring with a volume that had been published only three weeks earlier and his claim to have been fighting single-handed for the same views suggests that he had been doing so for longer than that. Nevertheless, the letter to Tocqueville remains significant as a crucial step on the way to the argument of *On Liberty*, particularly in its concern for resistance to the tendencies of mass society. Tocqueville, then, though not the source of these ideas, certainly reinforced and, through his immense prestige, validated them. This is more than confirmed by the points Mill made in his 1840 *Edinburgh Review* article on Tocqueville's second volume. In a summary of the volume Mill noted that 'Chinese stationariness' was a particular danger to society advancing towards 'equality of condition'. The assertion of a link between democracy and stagnation could, of course, be taken as part of an anti-democratic argument and so used in opposition to the egalitarian trend. This would appear to let England off the hook. Mill, however, rejected this application. He believed that exactly the same trends were 'in full operation in aristocratic England'.[25]

The next significant treatment of this theme appeared in Mill's article on 'Guizot's Essays and Lectures on History', which were published in the *Edinburgh Review* of October 1845 (and will be treated more fully in the next section). Mill noted Guizot's point that earlier despotisms had become stationary through their one basic principle having rapidly worked itself out. He then broke through the satisfying divide between them and us – the single-track despotisms of the East and the diverse and complex civilization of Europe – to warn again that our fate might be similar to theirs. Stationary despotism was not 'a danger existing only in the past; but one which may be yet impending over the future'. Mill warned that we might too easily have assumed that progress was 'an inherent property of our species'.

Education, for example – mental culture – would seem to have a better title than could be derived from anything else, to rule the world with exclusive authority; yet if the lettered and cultivated class, embodied and disciplined under a central organ, could become in Europe, what it is in China, the Government – unchecked by any power residing in the mass of citizens, and permitted to assume a parental tutelage over all the operations of life – the result would probably be a darker despotism, one more opposed to improvement, than even the military monarchies and aristocracies have in fact proved.

Mill then suggested that if current trends continued in the United States, 'the condition of human nature would become as stationary as in China'.[26]

Mill's most developed and best-known argument on China as a warning to the West is in Chapter Three of *On Liberty*. Here Mill moved from his focus on individual self-development to the more global issue of how Europe had elevated itself above the rest of mankind. China now appears as the supreme example of a characteristic of the *whole* East. Mill noted that civilization had died out in the Byzantine Empire and also that the 'greater part of the world has, properly speaking, no history, because the despotism of Custom is complete. This is the case over the whole East.'[27] Mill assumed that those 'nations *must* [emphasis added] once have had' the originality' that made them 'the greatest and most powerful nations of the world', but they were only 'progressive for a certain length of time'. They ground to a halt when they ceased to possess individuality' and we 'have a warning example in China – a nation of much talent', but 'they have become stationary – have remained so for thousands of years'.

In Mill's view the European nations had become 'an improving, instead of a stationary portion of mankind' because of their 'remarkable diversity of character and culture'. Europe, he believed, was '*wholly* indebted to this plurality of paths for its progressive and many-sided development'. We should note both that individual freedom has now become the sole means to national greatness and also that the mention of our cultural achievements is introduced for purposes of admonition rather than congratulation, for Europe was squandering its inheritance. It 'already begins to possess this benefit in a considerably less degree. It is decidedly advancing towards the Chinese ideal of making all people alike.' Mill drew on Wilhelm von Humboldt for two pre-conditions 'of human development, because necessary to render people unlike one another; namely, freedom, and variety of situations'. The first of these seemed not to be highly valued by the mass, while the 'second of these two conditions is *in this country* every day diminishing'. The obvious conclusion is that the cultural and social pre-conditions of human development were already severely weakened. It would obviously take some quite powerful and remarkable force to restore the situation.[28]

One well-known commentary has sought to separate out *On Liberty* from Mill's other writings.[29] On the estimate of China, however, and on its role as a significant example, Mill remained fairly consistent both before and after the publication of *On Liberty* in 1859. In *Considerations on Representative Government*, published two years later, he mentioned forms of government suitable for carrying a people beyond the level of savages but not for 'the step next beyond'. This situation was both frequent and among the 'most melancholy facts in history. The Egyptian hierarchy, the paternal despotism of China' are presented as 'very fit instruments for carrying those nations up to the point of civilization which they attained'. But there they were stuck. Further improvement stopped as 'they were brought to a permanent halt for want of mental liberty and individuality'.[30] Note that here Mill came near to referring to China and Egypt as civilizations. Their attainments and advances, limited though Mill thought they were, were still acknowledged in a way that he never did for India.

Two chapters later China was categorized with Russia as an example of 'both the good and bad side of bureaucracy'. The good side was 'fixed maxims, directed with Roman perseverance to the same unflinchingly-pursued ends from age to age' and also 'the remarkable skill with which those ends are generally pursued'. The negative side included 'the permanent organized hostility to improvements from without, which even the autocratic power of a vigorous-minded Emperor is seldom or never sufficient to overcome'.[31]

We have dealt with the depiction of China in the period that concerns us, and noted the uses to which that negative image could be put. It might now be worthwhile to ask briefly whether the nineteenth-century European perspective has been validated by historians nearer to our own time. In an immensely influential work of comparative historical sociology Barrington Moore, Jr noted that 'Modern sinologists are prone to deny that Chinese history has been fundamentally unchanged for two thousand years, asserting that this is an illusion due to our ignorance.' He, however, remained unconvinced, maintaining that to a 'nonspecialist it seems quite obvious that, in comparison with Europe, Chinese civilization did remain largely static. What changes are there in China comparable to the Western sequence of city state, world empire, feudalism, royal absolutism, and modern industrial society?'[32] Similarly, in the 1980s the Chinese scholar Wen-yuan Qian accepted that his country had lacked the 'propitious political-social conditions to produce, sustain and promote … a series of totally new intellectual elements, new attitudes, new ways of thinking' comparable to those of Europe.[33]

One final point about China needs to be made. This concerns its relationship with Britain at the time Mill was writing. In one sense the use of China as a warning was a rather distant example. For Mill and his contemporaries, however, it was highly pertinent in ways not yet mentioned. For a global

101

trading nation the whole world was of direct concern and in the years when *On Liberty* was written and published, Great Britain was actually at war with China and had, as a result of China's attempts to stamp out the opium trade, been in dispute with it for over two decades. The first opium war lasted from 1839 to 1842, at which time the Treaty of Nanking gave Britain the port of Hong Kong and rights of access to five Chinese ports, 'a concession hitherto denied to foreign traders'.[34] Further trading disagreements led to the second opium war between 1856 and 1860. This began when the Chinese police in Canton seized what they took to be a pirate ship, the *Arrow*, and arrested its Chinese crew. The British protested, possibly wrongly, that the ship had been flying the British flag, and insisted on an apology and the release of the crew. The Chinese refused and so the Governor of Hong Kong sent 'British warships to destroy Chinese fortifications and to bombard Canton'. The Governor was well known to Mill. He was none other than Sir John Bowring, a founding member of the Anti-Corn Law League, former radical MP, former supporter of the Chartists, former editor of the *Westminster Review* and 'a close friend of Jeremy Bentham (Bentham died in his arms)', who, 'as his literary executor, had edited his eleven-volume *Collected Works*'.[35]

Mill's only recorded comment on the bombardment of Canton was in a letter to Edwin Chadwick, former secretary to Jeremy Bentham, but best known for his influential 1842 *Report on the Sanitary Condition of the Labouring Population of Great Britain*. In March 1857, five months after the seizure of the *Arrow*, Mill confided that he had not made himself 'conversant with the details'. This, however, did not deter him from a somewhat intemperate defence of Bowring which involved relegating the Chinese to the category of barbarian that the Celestial Empire itself imposed on all others. The letter is also a clear forerunner of 'A Few Words on Non-intervention', of two years later, which was discussed in Chapter 3, Part IV:

> What disgusted me was the stupidity (if it was no worse) of supposing that people here could judge of the effect that would be produced on the minds of barbarians who put to death several thousands per year by the more or less of reparation demanded where some was evidently due; the ridiculous appeals to humanity and Christianity in favour of ruffians, & to international law in favour of people who recognize no laws of war at all (witness the poisonings and stabbings in the back) & the attempt to make our Bowring a 'flagitious' liar.[36]

The issues involved relate closely to both liberalism and imperialism. In its economic aspect liberalism is closely identified with free trade. This policy, then, had to be imposed internationally and so, as Eric Hobsbawm has pointed out, 'any countries which did not care to enter into relations with the advanced world, that is largely with Britain, were forced to do so by gunboats and marines';[37] they were, if not 'forced to be free', then to adapt Rousseau's phrase, forced to be free traders. On some accounts the East India Company was at the forefront of what is now called globalization. Attempts to trade with China had long been beset with difficulties. The Chinese standpoint had been made particularly clear years earlier, in 1793, when the Emperor Kienlung had told an envoy from King George III that 'since our celestial Empire possesses all things in prolific abundance and lacks no products within its borders' it had 'no need to import the manufactures of outside barbarians in exchange for our own products'.[38] The two opium wars, however, forced China into commerce with the modern economies of the West. Mid-way between them Karl Marx noted how the bourgeoisie 'draws all, even the most barbarian, nations into civilisation. The cheap price of its commodities are the heavy artillery with which it batters down all Chinese walls, with which it forces the barbarians' intensely obstinate hatred of foreigners to capitulate.'[39] Clearly, the Emperor and the revolutionary had different notions as to who was civilized and who wasn't. Clearly also, the metaphor of the *Communist Manifesto* became more literal as, ultimately, trade on its own was unable to enforce capitulation without the actual assistance of gunboats.

Attempts to force a trading connection on to China, and on to Japan, were proceeding while Mill was closely following and commenting on political events. This period was also his last two decades of employment with the British East India Company. This is of direct relevance because the enforced sale of opium to the Chinese provided, according to John Newsinger, 'the British administration in India's second most important source of revenue and, for the first two thirds of the nineteenth century, its most important export'.[40] According to another source, 'opium yielded one seventh of the total revenue of British India in the nineteenth century. The China trade was essential to the prosperity of the British Empire.'[41] If the East India Company was at least partially dependent on the forcing on to the Chinese market of opium manufactured in British India then, indirectly, the same might be true of Mill's own position and income.

The British politician most associated with the pursuit of the opium wars was Lord Palmerston, who was Foreign Secretary during the first and Prime Minister for most of the second. In 1850 Palmerston had made his position clear. He announced that the time was coming

> when we shall be obliged to strike another blow in China ... These half-civilized Governments such as those of China, Portugal, Spanish America, all require a dressing every eight or ten years to keep them in order. Their minds are too shallow to receive an impression that will last longer than some such period ... they must not only see the stick but actually feel it on their shoulders.[42]

The other side, unusually, united Gladstone and Cobden with Disraeli. During the first opium war Gladstone conceded that 'we, the enlightened and civilized Christians, are pursuing objects at variance both with justice and religion'.[43] Disraeli also raised the issue of civilization in a parliamentary debate during the second opium war: 'You have been reminded in this debate that China enjoys a civilization of twenty-five centuries. In point of antiquity the civilization of Europe is nothing to that.'[44] Meanwhile Mill's public silence on this issue, when so vocal on so many others, speaks volumes. Free trade clearly comes first.

So, for the first readers of *On Liberty*, China was the current enemy and Mill's use of it as a symbol of recalcitrant backwardness would have had a powerful emotional force that has since been neglected. This situation is never made apparent in the normal decontextualized commentary on Mill's writings, yet brief mention of the opium trade issue was made in Chapter Five of *On Liberty*. There, in a regrettably convoluted section, Mill was discussing the relationship between individual liberty and free trade. He pointed out how the advantages of free trade were conceded only 'after a long struggle' and that in general 'Restrictions on trade, or on production for purposes of trade, are indeed restraints; and all restraints, *qua* restraint, is an evil.' The extent of the doctrine, however, was limited so as to allow the authorities to prevent 'fraud by adulteration' and to enforce 'sanitary precautions' and 'to protect workpeople employed in dangerous occupations'. Mill then turned to another category of interference where the liberty of the buyer made restriction unacceptable. Here he included both the sale of poisons and 'the importation of opium into China'.[45] Mill had also mentioned this issue in a memorandum of 1858, so presumably written around the time when the finishing touches were being put to *On Liberty*. Here he denied that the sale of opium had been 'an improper source of revenue' for the East India Company.[46] Its sale and consumption was, after all, legal in Britain at that time. Mill, then, presumably, was on Palmerston's side in his desire to force opium on to the Chinese market. Certainly if one took the bare facts of the opium wars in isolation from other factors concerning the two countries, the conclusion as to which of them was the more civilized might not seem as obvious as Mill presumed.

THE CAUSES OF STAGNATION

Mill's most famous warning of stagnation at home comes, of course, in *On Liberty*, to which we shall turn shortly. The concerns voiced there, however, had been with Mill a long time. 'The Spirit of the Age' articles of 1831 already indicate his awareness of the issue. As a Benthamite Mill was brought up to be critical of the aristocracy and inclined to the view that unchallengeable power can lead to stagnation. The British upper classes, he decided, had lost the benefits of an 'invigorating atmosphere' and so 'have retrograded in all the higher qualities of mind'. Mill's studies of antiquity confirmed this as a general historical tendency for the 'decline of the ancient commonwealths' demonstrated that 'luxury deadens and enervates the mind'. Further, as an agnostic, Mill was keen to note the power of religious orthodoxy in holding societies back. He noted that 'religion possesses a sufficient ascendancy, to subdue the minds of the possessors of worldly power'. This was the case 'among two great stationary communities – the Hindoos and the Turks' and was 'the chief cause which keeps those communities stationary'.[47]

A particularly strong influence on Mill was François Guizot, the French historian and statesman, whose histories of Europe and of France Mill discussed jointly in the *London Review* of 1836 and singly and at more length in the *Edinburgh Review* of October 1845. In a comment that clearly foreshadows the emphasis on diversity in *On Liberty*, he agreed with Guizot that the development of European civilization had been unique in the continual existence of 'rival powers naturally tending in different directions'.[48] This had made its development slower than that of other civilizations, but also advantageous in being more durable. Guizot believed that other civilizations, in contrast, had developed to the full the one single principle on which they were based, but had then stagnated. 'In Asia, for example, one class completely triumphed, and the government of castes succeeded to that of classes, and society sunk into immobility. Thank God, none of this has happened in Europe.'[49] That last sentence was to be taken literally, for Guizot did in fact attribute Europe's good fortune to divine intercession. 'European civilization … progresses according to the intentions of God.' Furthermore – and it was nice of a Frenchman to note this – England seemed to have been particularly blessed. 'So,' Guizot continued, 'the essence of liberty is the manifestation and simultaneous action of all interests, rights, powers, and social elements. England was therefore much nearer its possession than the majority of other states.' Over the course of English history no ancient principle had ever been entirely lost nor modern one wholly victorious. 'There has always been a simultaneous development of different forces.'[50] Mill, in contrast, was not disposed to see his own country as an example of anything having been done properly. He was also less triumphalist and less assured of Europe's immunity from the tendencies that had impeded less fortunate cultures. It was Guizot's analysis of the negative aspects of backward cultures rather than the advantages of his own that made the greatest impression on Mill.

Guizot's *History of Civilization in Europe* (1828), then, was overwhelmingly positive in its assessment. In slight but still significant contrast *The History of Civilization in France* contains some warning signs. It was published between 1829 and 1832, that is over the time of the 1830 revolution, a situation that might well have induced certain doubts. From Volume Four Mill extracted a section in which individuality was said to have declined below the level characteristic of the feudal epoch. Presumably Guizot was distancing himself from the ideas of the Enlightenment when he wrote that France 'had lived for half a century under the empire of general ideas, more and more accredited and powerful; and under the pressure of formidable, almost irresistible events'. These ideas and events seem to have had distinct disadvantages, for there had

> resulted a certain weakness, a certain effeminacy, in our minds and characters. Individual convictions and will are wanting in energy and confidence in themselves. Men assent to a prevailing opinion, obey a general impulse, yield to an external necessity. Whether for resistance or for action, each has but a mean idea of his own strength, a feeble reliance on his own judgement. Individuality, the inward and personal energy of man, is weak and timid. Amidst the progress of public liberty, many seem to have lost the proud and invigorating sentiment of their own personal liberty.[51]

Much has been made of Tocqueville's influence on Mill but this passage, which breathes the same spirit as *On Liberty*, supports Georgios Varouxakis's view that Guizot's ideas were equally important.[52] Guizot further humiliated his own age by comparing it adversely with the middle ages in the one respect that then, 'in many persons, individuality was strong, will was energetic'.[53]

Even so, Guizot did not go so far as to see European society as under threat. This was the further step that Mill took in adapting Guizot's analysis of other cultures as a warning for his own. The chronology here is interesting. Mill's 1836 review of Guizot, written jointly with Joseph Blanco White, contains no intimation of this development.[54] This came first in Mill's 1840 review of Tocqueville's second volume of *Democracy in America*. Here Mill explicitly mentioned Guizot as the source of the idea that lack of diversity led to a condition in which communities 'came to a halt, and became immoveable'. He then went beyond Guizot in adding that it 'would be an error to suppose that such could not possibly be our fate'. Mill warned that with the 'complete preponderance' of the 'spirit of industry and commerce' society would be dominated by a single orthodoxy and so might move into 'an era either of stationariness or of decline'.[55] The point was reiterated in Mill's 1845 review. After discussing Guizot on 'the great stationary despotisms of the East', Mill warned:

> Nor is this a danger existing only in the past; but one which may be yet impending over the future. If the perpetual antagonism which has kept the human mind alive, were to give place to the complete preponderance of any, even the most salutary, element, we might yet find that we have counted too confidently upon the progressiveness which we are so often told is an inherent property of our species.

Mill certainly favoured education as much as almost anything else that comes to mind, but even an educated stratum enjoying unchecked power, as in China, could become despotic. Similarly in the United States if the mass were able to silence all unorthodox opinion then 'the condition of human nature would become as stationary as China'.[56] Here, then, fourteen years earlier, we find much of the argument concerning the basis of progress that Mill was to forward in *On Liberty*.

When Guizot gave the lectures that became *The History of Civilization in Europe* Alexis de Tocqueville was among the audience. In the Introduction to the Penguin Books edition Larry Siedentop says that Tocqueville's 'enthusiasm for them knew no bounds'. Tocqueville himself wrote that Guizot's work was 'prodigious in its analysis of ideas and choice of words, truly prodigious'.[57] Though both believed that Europe's superiority was providentially determined, there were clear differences between them. Guizot saw Europe as in the forefront on civilization whereas Tocqueville emphasized its advance to democracy. Guizot was the theorist of how *other* civilizations stagnate, Tocqueville of the dangers facing his own. Consequently Tocqueville was less complacent concerning the survival of freedom. For him democracy might well combine with freedom but, on balance, was more likely to endanger it. Tocqueville's focus was more sociological, emphasizing the extent to which diversity in ideas depended upon a differentiated social structure. Guizot was more concerned with the power of ideas and institutions in creating and enforcing orthodoxies. Mill learnt a lot from both of them and combined Guizot's theory of social change and stagnation with Tocqueville's of mass society and conformity.

Fourteen years divide Mill's second Guizot review from the publication of *On Liberty*. During those years it is clear that the concerns voiced in both works remained in Mill's mind. In the introduction to Volume XI of Mill's *Collected Works*, F. E. Sparshott noted that the 'degeneracy of modern man is a recurrent theme in Mill's correspondence about this time'.[58] He was referring particularly to 1849, the year in which Mill found an especially striking remark in his friend George Grote's *History of Greece*. Grote believed that no modern government could match the tolerance of dissent found in the speeches of Athenian statesmen. In modern times, said Grote, the 'intolerance of the national opinion cuts down individual character to one out of a few set types, to which every person, or every family, is constrained to adjust itself, and beyond which all exceptions meet either with hatred or derision'.

Immediately after copying this out Mill added: 'There have been few things lately written more worthy of being meditated on than this striking paragraph.' He then referred to 'the comparative mediocrity of modern times'.[59] A year later, in the aftermath of the uprisings of 1848–49, Mill's mood was particularly gloomy. 'We have come', he thought, 'to a period, when progress, even of a political kind, is coming to a halt, by reason of the low intellectual & moral state of all classes: of the rich as much as of the poorer classes.'[60]

Though the themes of *On Liberty* had clearly been emerging for many years previously, the first draft was written in 1854. The decision to convert that short essay into a book is recorded in a letter that Mill wrote to Harriet Mill from Rome on 15 January 1855:

> On my way here cogitating thereon I came back to an idea we have talked about & thought that the best thing to write & publish at present would be a volume on Liberty. So many things might be brought into it & nothing seems to me more needed – it is a growing need too, for opinion tends to encroach more & more on liberty, & almost all the projects of social reformers in these days are really liberticide – Comte, particularly so.[61]

This is a striking confession. Twenty years earlier, in essays we have already discussed, Mill had sought to place himself between the traditions of the Enlightenment and its opponents, or, as he personalized it, between Bentham and Coleridge. His own upbringing, of course, aligned him with the former in each of these pairings, though he hoped to integrate what was of value in the latter. Furthermore, Mill had welcomed the French revolutions of 1830 and 1848, a position not calculated to increase his popularity in England. He had also been much influenced by the Saint-Simonians and spoken in favour of Fourier. But now he amalgamates nearly all social reformers with Comte and 'liberticide'! Mill had been no supporter of conservatism but here, in distancing himself from the radicals, the very people most associated with projects of improvement, he seemed to be verifying the analysis not just of Tocqueville but of all the defenders of the *ancien régime*; all those who argued that the revolution and modernity had undermined freedom rather than extending it.

In *On Liberty* Mill argued that all improvements in the institutions and mind of Europe could be traced back to three periods of free intellectual ferment. One was the period immediately following the Reformation. Another was the Enlightenment, which Mill described as 'limited to the Continent'. If, as was common, this implicitly excluded England, then Mill would be denigrating the Benthamite influence that had dominated his own upbringing.[62] Mill's third instance was 'the intellectual fermentation of Germany during the Goethian and Fichtean period'.[63] Though two of these instances were comparatively recent, Mill felt that their influence was coming to an end. 'Appearances have for some time indicated that all three impulses are well nigh spent.'[64]

In the same year that Mill wrote the first draft of *On Liberty* an English translation of William von Humboldt's *The Sphere and Duties of Government* was published, over half a century after its first German printing. Mill acknowledged Humboldt's significance by quoting him in the frontspiece of the book: 'The grand, leading principle, towards which every argument unfolded in these pages directly converges, is the absolute and essential importance of human development in its richest diversity.'[65] This, however, was very much the opposite of what seemed to be occurring. It was not only that individuality was in decline but that additionally this process seemed scarcely a cause for concern. Most people remained 'satisfied with the ways of mankind as they now are'.[66] Society, then, had 'now fairly got the better of individuality' and was exercising a form of collective control that was gradually undermining the very inclination to be different. 'In our times,' thought Mill, 'from the highest class of society down to the lowest, every one lives as under the eye of a hostile and dreaded censorship.' Society had now so imposed itself on individuality that it no longer even occurred to people 'to have any inclination, except for what is customary. Thus the mind itself is bowed to the yoke.' This led to what Mill called the 'despotism of custom', which was 'everywhere the standing hindrance to human advancement'. The contest between liberty and custom, he thought, 'constitutes the chief interest of the history of mankind'.[67]

The problem was not merely a change in the mental condition of individuals; it was rather that their surrounding circumstances were being transformed. In a famous passage Mill traced the increasing homogeneity of society's various parts: 'The circumstances which surround different classes and individuals, and shape their characters, are daily becoming more assimilated. Formerly, different ranks, different neighbourhoods, different trades and professions, lived in what might be called different worlds; at present, to a great degree in the same.' Furthermore, this 'assimilation is still proceeding. *All* [emphasis added] the political changes of the age promote it, since they all tend to raise the low and to lower the high. Every extension of education promotes it'[68] though education was one thing that Mill consistently wanted extended. 'Improvement in the means of communication promote it … The increase of commerce and manufactures promotes it' as does 'the ascendancy of public opinion in the State'.[69] Clearly, then, the increase of similarity was being furthered by all the major tendencies of the time.

Contrary to the bulk of progressive opinion, it did not here seem to Mill that time had brought improvement. In earlier stages, even in the middle ages, which otherwise Mill was not disposed to praise, 'the individual was a power in himself'. This was no longer the case. Mediocrity was on the rise, gradually becoming the 'ascendant power among mankind'. Individuals, consequently, had become 'lost in the crowd' and the 'only power deserving the name is that of masses, and of governments while they make themselves the organ of the tendencies and instincts of masses'. In England the significant public was that of the middle class; in the United States of America, the 'whole white population', but either way they were 'always a mass, that is to

109

say, collective mediocrity'. Nor was this just an Anglo-Saxon problem, for 'the general tendency of things throughout the world is to render mediocrity the ascendant power among mankind'. A few pages later Mill returned home with the observation that the 'greatness of England is now all collective: individually small, we only appear capable of anything by our habit of combining'. He then turned to his prognosis of actual degeneration, warning that 'it was men of another stamp than this that made England what it has been; and men of another stamp will be needed to prevent its decline'.[70]

For Mill mass society stood in basic antagonism to social progress. It fortified what was customary and crushed 'that disposition to aim at something better'. It was the new enemy and so its victims could be caught off-guard. The old enemy was the state. Liberalism thus far had sought protection from the state by such means as the rule of law, human rights and government by consent. Mill's view now was that society itself was so flattened out that any individuality became highly visible and subject to suppression. Such a society had become the main threat to human freedom.

In contrast to the analysis in *Political Economy*, liberty for Mill now becomes 'the *only* unfailing and permanent source of improvement' and the contest between liberty and custom is said to constitute 'the chief interest of the history of mankind'.[71] In his most pessimistic account of his own society, Mill believed that the battle for liberty, and hence the struggle for continued global leadership, was being lost. If liberty loses – and on Mill's account it certainly seemed to be losing – civilization comes to a standstill. This is what the example of China was held to demonstrate. Mill then, to summarize, argued that Britain and Europe were not merely failing to sustain but were actually undermining the very foundations on which their global pre-eminence rested. This was the most fundamental charge Mill ever made against his own society. In comparison, his other concerns pale into relative insignificance.

This is a much more pessimistic analysis than that presented in Mill's 1840 review of Tocqueville's second volume, for now there 'ceases to be any social support for nonconformity – any substantive power in society, which, itself opposed to the ascendancy of numbers, is interested in taking under its protection opinions and tendencies at variance with those of the public'.[72] The obvious conclusion from this is that the cultural and social pre-conditions of human development were already severely weakened. Thus we cannot affirm John Gray's statement that Mill believed in 'the practical irreversibility of the condition of freedom'.[73] We have seen that for Mill nearly all the social forces of his time were operating in the same direction of undermining liberty. Mill's sociology, then, provides an inauspicious base for a politics of resistance. It would clearly take some quite powerful and remarkable force to restore the situation. The last paragraph of Chapter Three begins with what, in the context, seems a massive understatement: 'The combination of all these

STANDSTILL: THE CASE OF CHINA

causes forms so great a mass of influences hostile to Individuality, that it is not easy to see how it can stand its ground.'[74]

THE ETHIC OF RESISTANCE

Mill had suggested how social developments had produced a homogeneous and conformist society. Yet, clearly, he wrote more than an analysis of the causes and possible consequences of mass society, for he issued what amounts to a manifesto of spirited resistance to it. *On Liberty* is rightly taken as being a philosophical exercise but beyond that it is *also* a political manifesto and, I shall argue, its political purpose is fundamental and, hence, its philosophical exercise is secondary, a means to an end, the end being the improvement of society. This presentation depends very heavily upon the argument contained in Chapter Three: 'Of Individuality, as One of the Elements of Well-being'.

Mill himself said of *On Liberty* that 'None of my writings have been either so carefully composed, or so sedulously corrected as this.'[75] This has not been obvious to all readers, particularly in respect of the tone and placing of Chapter Three. Margaret Canovan believes that Chapter Three can be 'regarded as the heart of the book … it is in this chapter above all that the essay's message is most directly expressed'. Nevertheless she sees some problems about it and notes ways in which Mill's important third chapter is different from the others. First, it is different in tone. The dispassionate and somewhat aloof voice of the other chapters is replaced by a more polemical one; this shift being appropriate for a second one, the replacement of the philosopher by the campaigner: 'we seem instead to hear a different, more strident voice … his eloquence here is that of a partisan fighting openly for a cause'.[76]

Why, then, one might wonder, was Mill reluctant to campaign from the start of the book? If, as Canovan suggests, the 'detachment' was rhetorical, that is hiding a partisanship, why should such partisanship become open and explicit in Chapter Three when previously it was apparently best hidden? Canovan ponders three possible reasons without fully committing herself to any of them. At first sight Mill's shift seems like a change of tactics; one that would undermine the unity of the work as a whole. Canovan suggests, however, that this is not so, for Mill was engaged in a softening-up exercise in Chapters One and Two, where 'he takes care to appear as a detached observer'. Her argument continues, however, that this was just a rhetorical device. Mill 'goes to great lengths to get his readers on his side; he prepares the ground carefully before he makes radical statements'.[77] Having established himself as cool, sensible, logical, rational and somewhat aloof, he could then, on the basis of those credentials, sweep his readership into accepting the urgency of his main message.

This is an interesting suggestion with certainly some plausibility, though a counter-case could also be made. This would be that Mill did not need to provide two chapters to establish his credentials with his readership. These had already been well established over a decade earlier by his *Logic* and *Principles of Political Economy*. Furthermore it is hard to see such chapters as merely a ploy, as somehow not the real Mill, when in fact such a tone was Mill's normal mode, with, on the contrary, the polemical style being much less common within Mill's *oeuvre*. We must concede, however, that the issue of mass society and how to resist it is placed in a rather secondary position: at the end of Chapter Three, rather than at the beginning or end of the book.

Canovan's second suggestion draws heavily on an article by Richard Friedman which will concern us shortly. The argument here is that in the different chapters Mill was addressing different audiences; Chapter Three being distinctive in that it was addressed to the elite who will appreciate liberty for its own sake, rather than to the mass who might merely appreciate its consequences.[78]

Canovan's third suggestion, 'highly speculative but too interesting to neglect', is that in Chapter Three Harriet Taylor Mill's influence was particularly prominent, as the more strident and assertive style was characteristic of her writing. As evidence Canovan suggests that the 'subject matter' and 'to some degree' the tone of the chapter are similar to 'An Early Essay' written by Harriet Taylor in 1832.[79] This hypothesis is, of course, interesting in terms of the genesis of *On Liberty*, though it does not affect our main point here, that, in the words of John Day, the essay was 'not merely a moral and intellectual discourse, but also a passionate plea to his contemporaries to arrest the decline of individuality'.[80] That a misunderstanding could occur on this point and that it actually was a misunderstanding of Mill's intentions is more than confirmed by a letter he wrote to his friend Alexander Bain in August 1859, just six months after the book was first published.

> The 'Liberty' has produced an effect on you which it was never intended to produce if it has made you think that we ought not to attempt to convert the world. I meant nothing of the kind, & hold that we ought to convert all we can. We must be satisfied with keeping alive the sacred fire – in a few minds when we are unable to do more – but the notion of an intellectual aristocracy of lumières while the rest of the world remain in darkness fulfils none of my aspirations – & the effect I aim at by the book is, on the contrary, to make the many more accessible to all truth by making them more open minded.[81]

Turning now to the actual content of the book, let us ask what Mill thought could be done for society to regain freedom and diversity. What he required for further progress was the reassertion of individuality, for 'unless individuality shall be able successfully to assert itself against this yoke, Europe, notwithstanding its noble antecedents and its professed Christianity, will tend to become another China'.[82] As all great things come from individuals, so the fight back is of isolated individuals asserting their own particular identity. This is what Mill requires of them:

> It is in these circumstances most especially, that exceptional individuals, instead of being deterred, should be encouraged in acting differentially from the mass … In this age, the mere example of nonconformity, the mere refusal to bend the knee to custom, is itself a service … it is desirable, in order to break through that tyranny, that people should be eccentric … That so few now dare to be eccentric, marks the chief danger of the time.[83]

We have now, it is hoped, clarified both the problem and Mill's solution to it. In order to gauge the prospects for his tactics let us now note how he presents the balances of forces involved.

First, note that it is only 'exceptional individuals' whom Mill calls upon to act 'differentially'. In one sense this is definitional, in that acting differently of itself makes an individual exceptional. In a more significant sense, however, Mill is appealing to the 'more highly gifted and instructed One or Few'[84] to set an example for others to follow. John Day has noted:

> What emerges at this stage of the argument is that only a few people are capable of the kind of originality that Mill believes is so important in preventing human life becoming a 'stagnant pool'. Society, then, does not benefit particularly from the self-development of all or most of its members, but from the self-development of the small minority of geniuses that are capable of originality. Mill is placing the hopes of human progress on the achievements of a small intellectual, cultural and moral élite. It is their freedom to develop their individuality that is important for society.[85]

At this point it might appear that so long as the elite are imbued with the spirit of individuality, then progress would be secured. The solution is not that simple, however. Individuality, even for the few, is secure only when the wider society both facilitates and values it. This, thought Mill, was not the case. He noted that the majority were 'satisfied with the ways of mankind as they now are' and that 'the greatest difficulty to be encountered' lies 'in the indifference of persons in general to the end itself … the evil is, that individual spontaneity is hardly recognised by the common modes of thinking, as having any intrinsic worth, or deserving any regard on its own account'.[86] Mass society, it seems, is not opposed by the mass. Of themselves they don't value liberty but Mill hoped that he could win over the elite to the task of showing the masses their own real interest. The mass, then, constitute a 'difficulty', though Mill does not explain how the indifference of the mass is a threat to the educated few. For an explicit and convincing explanation we have to turn to Gertrude Himmelfarb. She has pointed out that 'the genius, then, was an object of special solicitude; it was his individuality that was most precious. But since he could only thrive in an "atmosphere of freedom", all men had to share the same degree of liberty. And they all had to share it for their own sakes as well as for the sake of genius.'[87] It now might appear that the mass are being asked to perform an act of altruism; that for the sake of the 'Few' the many should facilitate and tolerate a degree of individuality that they do not themselves value. What is needed, politically, is some kind of bargain by which the mass will be offered some benefit or reward for the freedom they allow to the few. This is the sense of Mill's belief that it was 'necessary further to show, that these developed human beings are of some use to the undeveloped – to point out to those who do not desire liberty, and would not avail themselves of it, that they may be in some intelligible manner rewarded for allowing other people to make use of it without hindrance'.[88] In my view the bargain is not convincingly set out by Mill, who failed to specify explicitly either what 'use' the 'developed human beings' are to the 'undeveloped' or the 'intelligible manner' in which the mass will be rewarded.

Richard Friedman, in an article that deserves to be better known, believes that Mill has made a clearer case than I have suggested. The core of Friedman's argument is that the freedom granted to the elite produces a level of progress from which all benefit. In his view 'the multitude are so strongly attracted to progress that they can be persuaded to accept its necessary condition, liberty, despite their aversion to liberty'. They gain what Friedman calls 'an instrumental allegiance to the principle of liberty'.[89] While it's not clear to me that this is what Mill does argue, I would suggest that even so the chances of persuasion are not good. Mill notes, for example, that 'Originality is the one thing which unoriginal minds cannot feel the use of. They cannot see what it is to do for them: how should they?' Additionally, in a passage that Friedman quotes, Mill estimates 'the state of feeling and opinion among the vulgar with regard to human liberty' and doesn't think much of it. 'So far from setting any value on individuality – so far from respecting the right of each individual to act, in things indifferent, as seems good to his own judgement and inclinations' they 'cannot conceive that a person in a state of sanity can desire such freedom'.[90] We may, then, suggest, that even at the ideological level, the task of education is enormous and that it is far from clear that Mill had found an agency capable of achieving it.

Our second general point on the balance of forces is not considered by Friedman at all. It is that, after a mass that doesn't want liberty, we have a society moving powerfully in the wrong direction. We have already noticed how, towards the end of Chapter Three of *On Liberty*, Mill suggested that 'All the political changes of the age'.[91] were leading towards mass society. From this one could plausibly conclude that the tendency was too inexorable to encourage fight back let alone give it a chance of victory.

In his review of Tocqueville's first volume of 1835 Mill had not regarded mass society as a danger to England. This confidence had noticeably declined when he reviewed the second volume in 1840. Here there is a decidedly more sociological and less individualist approach than we find later. Mill had speci-fied three groups who provided the bases of resistance, an approach not followed in *On Liberty* where he just called for 'individuals' to refuse to bend the knee. This seems a less promising tactic than to locate a propitious social grouping within society, whose solidarity might support each individual in strengthening their sub-cultural resistance to mass society. In the second review Mill also stressed the importance of a check on 'the unbalanced influ-ence of the commercial spirit', and linked the tyranny of the majority with the spirit of industry and commerce as something to be resisted. He also empha-sized the need for a countervailing influence to that of the commercial class.[92] In *On Liberty* Mill did not repeat this explicit linking of mass society with capitalism, nor did he mention social and institutional bases of resistance to mass society; in 1859 only the recalcitrant individual remained as a possible countervailing power.

Success is rendered even less likely by the disaggregation of the forces opposed to mass society. With all great things apparently coming from the individual, it is unsurprising that the vital fight back against mass society is undertaken by spirited and intelligent individuals 'refusing to bend the knee' and battling alone. 'The initiation of all wise or noble things, comes and must come from individuals; generally at first from some one individual.'[93] No pressure group or political party is suggested in opposition to the dominant trends. This lack of aggregation renders Mill's forces weaker than their combined strength might make them. It reinforces the sense that Mill was, unwittingly of course, encouraging futile gestures. His solitary individual refusing to bend the knee would be swept away by the force of the mass heading in the wrong direction. We must, then, note the inadequacy of Mill's proposals in terms of the problem he outlines. In short, what he wants is overcome by what he describes and so his sociology undermines his ethics.

In the face of the numerous major social forces inexorably crushing individuality, Mill's final appeal on the issue, calling on 'the intelligent part of the public to feel [individuality's] value', comes over as particularly tame. He says that if 'the claims of Individuality are ever to be asserted, the time is now, while much is still wanting to complete the enforced assimilation. It is only in the early stages that any stand can be successfully made against the encroachment'. After that, 'Mankind speedily become unable to conceive diversity, when they have been for some time unaccustomed to see it.'[94] So here, after all that has gone before, we are to presume that society was still in the 'early stages' of its ossification, although the description given previously, and the tone of urgency in which it was done, suggested a later stage of degeneration. So, although Mill's call was still for resistance there is in the mood at the end of our key chapter an atmosphere of post-mortem for the glory that once was.

Gertrude Himmelfarb has described it as 'curious how little attention [Mill] paid to this book after it was published ... his correspondence is remarkably sparse on the subject of *On Liberty*, or indeed on the subject of liberty in general'.[95] From Mill's letters of the 1859–60 period it seems that parliamentary reform and Hare's scheme of proportional representation were the issues that most preoccupied him. Furthermore, Himmelfarb mentions that in his *Autobiography*, written 'during the same years as *On Liberty*',[96] Mill mentioned the 'great advance in liberty of discussion' since his childhood.[97] Himmelfarb's concern was to argue for two J. S. Mills by separating out *On Liberty* from the other writings.[98] Our endeavour has been nearly the opposite: to show how the work that Mill rightly foresaw as the one which would survive longest of his writings connects with the rest of them. In this respect we can indicate that in his *Autobiography* Mill defended *On Liberty* by attributing to merely 'superficial observation' the view that its message was not needed. The current tolerance was held to be a particularity of eras of transition. It is when new norms have established themselves that the 'teachings of the *Liberty* will have their greatest value. And it is to be feared that they will retain that value a long time.'[99]

Mill's *Considerations on Representative Government* were published in 1861, just two years after *On Liberty*, and in it there are a number of connections with the earlier work. There is, for example, in the second chapter, a long passage which most clearly reiterates the mood of pessimism we noted in Chapter Three of *On Liberty*. Once again Mill has the few trying to hold back the forces of deterioration. He described how, in antiquity, politics was 'an unceasing struggle against causes of deterioration; *as it even now is* [emphasis added]'. Mill noted that though people had come to believe in a tendency towards improvement, they ought 'not to forget, that there is an incessant and ever-flowing current of human affairs towards the worse, consisting of all the follies, all the vices, all the negligences, indolences, and supineness of mankind'. This counter-current was only kept under control by the efforts of some people to pursue 'good and worthy objects'. Nevertheless, the situation remained so precarious that even a 'very small diminution of those exertions' would bring improvement to a halt and 'turn the general tendency of things towards deterioration'. Appalling though this was, Mill's imagination had still not reached its nadir. He here imagined Western society on a downward spiral turning with increased velocity and so 'more and more difficult to check', until it eventually fell back into the condition from which it had so long previously emerged: the situation 'in which many large portions of mankind even now grovel; when hardly anything short of super-human power seems sufficient to turn the tide, and give afresh commencement to the upward movement'.[100]

Later in the same work Mill reiterated his view that the 'natural tendency of representative government, as of modern civilization, is towards collective mediocrity'. He then drew on the points he had learnt from Guizot, that continual progress is dependent on antagonism, and it was on this basis that he worked tirelessly in support of Thomas Hare's scheme of proportional representation. This method of election would provide what representative democracy otherwise lacked, 'a *point d'appui*, for individual resistance to the tendencies of the ruling power'.[101] Thus, what to some seems merely a turn to the mechanics of constitutional arrangements was in fact intimately linked to Mill's continuing sociological and philosophical concerns with the most threatening tendencies of modern society.

This concern with diversity is also found in Mill's 'Chapter on Socialism', written in 1869 and published posthumously ten years later. In discussing 'Communist associations' Mill struck the now familiar pessimistic note in stating that the 'obstacles to human progression are always great ... but an indispensable condition of their being overcome is, that human nature should have freedom to expand spontaneously in various direction, both in thought and practice'. Mill then said that people should not allow their rulers to do their thinking for them nor tell them how to act. In communist societies this warning would be particularly important, for there the control exercised by the public authorities would leave even less scope for individuality than has existed under other advanced societies. As it was, even without communism, 'the compression of individuality by the majority is a great and growing evil'.[102]

We have, then, now covered our main theme of Mill's pessimistic analysis of developments in a society that on many criteria seemed remarkably successful. It just remains to consider how his account was seen by his contemporaries and by ours before considering where our inquiry leaves Mill's reputation as a liberal thinker.

NOTES

1. 'Crucial terms such as "East", "Orient", and "West" became devices for reducing endless complexities and diversities into manageable and falsifying unities.' J. J. Clarke, *Oriental Enlightenment. The Encounter Between Asian and Western Thought* (London: Routledge, 1997), p. 10. See also, of course, E. W. Said, *Orientalism* (Harmondsworth: Penguin Books, 1991), which deals with the same basic issue, although its examples are mainly from the Near East.
2. Montesquieu, *The Spirit of the Laws* [1748] (Cambridge: Cambridge University Press, 1989), p. 235.
3. *Edinburgh Review*, 1834, pp. lix, 362–5.
4. Clarke, *Oriental Enlightenment*, p. 73.

5. W. Bagehot, *Physics and Politics* [1872] (London: Kegan Paul, n.d.), p. 53.
6. Quoted in E. Stokes, *The English Utilitarians and India* (Delhi: Oxford University Press, 1992), p. 33.
7. Thus in terms of Mill's categorizations it is wrong to assume that he places China and India as similarly backward, as is done, for example, by B. Baum in *Rereading Power and Freedom in J. S. Mill* (Toronto: Toronto University Press, 2000), pp. 17, 58.
8. Emphasis added. Clarke, *Oriental Enlightenment*, p. 49. See also R. Dawson (ed.), *The Legacy of China* (Oxford: Clarendon Press, 1964), ch. 1, 'Western Conceptions of Chinese Civilization'.
9. Voltaire, *The Age of Louis XIV and Other Selected Writings* (London: The New English Library, 1966), p. 285.
10. M. de Condorcet, *Outlines of an Historical View of the Progress of the Human Mind* (London: J. Johnson, 1795), pp. 66, 67.
11. Quoted in Jonathan D. Spence, *The Great Chan's Continent: China in Western Minds* (New York: Norton, 1998), pp. 99, 100.
12. B. Parekh (ed.), *Bentham's Political Thought* (London: Croom Helm, 1973), p. 233.
13. V. G. Kiernan, *The Lords of Human Kind: European Attitudes to the Outside World in the Imperial Age* (Harmondsworth: Penguin Books, 1972), p. 155.
14. Quoted in Burrow, *Whigs and Liberals: Continuity and Change in English Political Thought* (Oxford: Clarendon, 1988), p. 121. See also pp. 87, 116.
15. A. Smith, *The Wealth of Nations* [1776] (Harmondsworth: Penguin Books, 1973), p. 174; see also p. 295.
16. T. Malthus, *An Essay on the Principle of Population* [1798] (Harmondsworth: Penguin Books, 1970), p. 191.
17. James Mill, 'Review of "Voyages à Peking, Manille, et l'Ile de France, faits dans l'Intervalle des Années 1784 à 1801" by M. De Guignes', *Edinburgh Review*, July 1809, vol. 14, pp. 407–29, 413–14, 424.
18. G. W. F. Hegel, *Philosophy of History* (New York: Dover Publications, 1956), pp. 99, 116. See also pp. 101, 105–6. Also see B. Constant, *Political Writings*, ed. B. Fontana (Cambridge: Cambridge University Press, 1988), p. 125; H. Maine, *Ancient Law* [1861] (London: Dent, 1954), p. 14.
19. K. Marx and F. Engels, *Articles on Britain* (Moscow: Progress Publishers, 1975), p. 272 and see the same book for similar remarks on India, a reminder that the wider context of the China syndrome is that the whole Orient seemed stagnant.
20. *Marx Engels Collected Works*, vol. 16 (London: Lawrence and Wishart, 1980), p. 16 and vol. 19 (London: Lawrence and Wishart, 1984), p. 216 from 'Chinese Affairs' published in *Die Presse*, 7 July1862. See also the discussion of 'Asiatic society' in T. Bottomore et al., *A Dictionary of Marxist Thought* (Oxford: Blackwell, 1985).
21. B. Constant, *Political Writings*, ed. B. Fontana (Cambridge: Cambridge University Press, 1988), p. 125.
22. A. de Tocqueville, *Democracy in America* (New York: Vintage Books, n.d.), vol. 2, pp. 3, 59, 78, 36, 48–9.
23. Letter of 11 May 1840, MCW, XIII, p. 434. Emphasis added.
24. MCW, X, p. 108.
25. MCW, XVIII, pp. 188, 196.
26. MCW, XX, p. 270.
27. *On Liberty*, p. 70; see also p. 65.

28. Emphasis added. *On Liberty*, pp. 70–2.
29. See G. Himmelfarb, *On Liberty and Liberalism: The Case of John Stuart Mill* (New York: Knopf, 1974), pp. xi, 73, 166, 257f., 338.
30. MCW, XIX, p. 396.
31. Ibid., p. 439.
32. Barrington Moore, Jr, *Social Origins of Dictatorship and Democracy* (Harmondsworth: Penguin Books, 1969), p.171, fn 16.
33. Quoted in J. J. Clarke, *Oriental Enlightenment*, p. 34.
34. E. J. Evans, *The Forging of the Modern State: Early Industrial Britain 1783–1870* (London: Longman, 1983), p. 202.
35. J. Newsinger, 'Elgin in China', *New Left Review*, 15, second series, May–June 2002, p. 126.
36. MCW, XV, p. 528.
37. Eric Hobsbawm, *Industry and Empire* (Harmondsworth: Penguin Books, 1969), p. 139.
38. Quoted in D. Bonner-Smith and W. W. R. Lumby (eds), *The Second China War 1856–1860* (London: Navy Records Society, 1954), pp. x–xi.
39. *Marx Engels Collected Works*, vol. 6 (London: Lawrence and Wishart, 1976), p. 488.
40. Newsinger, 'Elgin in China', p. 125. See also MCW, XXX, pp. 104–6.
41. P. R. Headrick, *The Tools of Empire. Technology and European Imperialism in the Nineteenth Century* (New York: Oxford University Press, 1981), p. 45.
42. Quoted in Newsinger, 'Elgin in China', p. 127.
43. P. Magnus, *Gladstone: A Biography* (London: John Murray, 1963), p. 52.
44. *Hansard*, 3 March 1857, col. 1837.
45. *On Liberty*, pp. 95, 96.
46. MCW, XXX, p. 106.
47. MCW, XXII, pp. 279, 305.
48. MCW, XX, p. 269.
49. Guizot, *The History of Civilization in Europe* [1828] (Harmondsworth: Penguin Books, 1997), p. 130; see also p. 15.
50. Ibid., pp. 32, 230, 229.
51. Quoted in MCW, XX, p. 286.
52. See G. Varouxakis, 'Guizot's Historical Works and J. S. Mill's Reception of Tocqueville', *History of Political Thought*, XX (2), Summer 1999, pp. 292–312.
53. MCW, XX, p. 286.
54. See MCW, XX, pp. 367–93.
55. MCW, XVIII, p. 197.
56. MCW, XX, p. 270.
57. Introduction to Guizot, *History of Civilization in Europe*, p. xxxi.
58. MCW, XI, p. xxxv, fn 113.
59. MCW, XXV, p. 1131.
60. MCW, XIV, p. 45.
61. Ibid., p. 294.
62. For a refutation of the view that the Enlightenment was basically confined to the European mainland, see Roy Porter, *Enlightenment: Britain and the Creation of the Modern World* (Harmondsworth: Penguin Books, 2001).
63. This third period is explained in MCW, I, p. 260.

64. *On Liberty*, p. 36.
65. Ibid., p. 3.
66. Ibid., p. 57 and see fn 68–9.
67. Ibid., pp. 61,70.
68. Compare Tocqueville's Introduction to Volume 1 of *Democracy in America*, p. 6.
69. *On Liberty*, pp. 72–3.
70. Ibid., pp.66, 70.
71. Emphasis added. Ibid., p. 70.
72. Ibid., p. 73.
73. John Gray, *Mill on Liberty: A Defence* (London: Routledge, 1996), p. 119; see also p. 120.
74. *On Liberty*, p. 73.
75. MCW, I, p. 249.
76. M. Canovan, 'The Eloquence of John Stuart Mill', *History of Political Thought*, VIII (3), Winter 1987, pp. 505–20, 515.
77. Ibid., pp. 509, 510.
78. See ibid., p. 518 and R. Friedman, 'A New Exploration of Mill's Essay *On Liberty*', *Political Studies*, XIV, 1966, pp. 281–304, esp. p. 304.
79. Canovan, 'The Eloquence of J. S. Mill', pp. 518, 519. Harriet's essay is reprinted as Appendix II of F. A. Hayek, *John Stuart Mill and Harriet Taylor: Their Friendship and Subsequent Marriage* (London: Routledge, 1951), pp. 275–9.
80. J. Day, 'John Stuart Mill: *On Liberty*' in M. Forsyth, M. Keens-Soper and J. Hoffman (eds), *The Political Classics. Hamilton to Mill* (Oxford: Oxford University Press, 1993), p. 225.
81. MCW, XV, p. 631.
82. *On Liberty*, p. 72.
83. Ibid., p. 67.
84. Ibid., p. 66. As usual, Mill's capitals are illuminating.
85. J. Day, 'John Stuart Mill: *On Liberty*', p. 223.
86. *On Liberty*, p. 57.
87. Himmelfarb, *On Liberty and Liberalism*, p. 67.
88. *On Liberty*, p. 64.
89. Friedman, 'A New Exploration', p. 301.
90. *On Liberty*, pp. 65, 69 fn.
91. Ibid., p. 73.
92. MCW, XVIII, p. 198.
93. *On Liberty*, p. 66.
94. Ibid., p. 74.
95. Himmelfarb, *On Liberty and Liberalism*, p. 268.
96. Ibid., p. 166.
97. MCW, I, p. 147.
98. See Himmelfarb, *On Liberty and Liberalism*, pp. xi, xix, 168.
99. MCW, I, p. 260.
100. MCW XIX, p. 388.
101. Ibid., pp. 457, 459.
102. MCW, V, p. 270.

Chapter Seven

Aftermath

MILL'S CONTEMPORARY CRITICS

Although *On Liberty* was published in the late 1850s, the formative period for its author was much earlier. Through his famous, severe and astonishingly sophisticated early education, one might suggest that Mill's mind was first formed in the 1810s; that is before his fourteenth birthday. In terms of our key chapter of *On Liberty*, however, we might suggest it shares some of the mood of pessimism of the 1835–49 period. These were years of bad harvests, economic depression, ongoing discontent with the first Reform Act and the Poor Law Amendment Act, growing urban squalor, the rise of Chartism, revolution in mainland Europe and fear of it in Great Britain. By 1859, however, when *On Liberty* was published, the general mood was more optimistic. Geoffrey Best voiced the historians' consensus when noting that the 'sense of safety after storms seems to have set in between 1848 and 1851' and that already by the latter date the 'hungry forties and the radical thirties suddenly seemed remote. The mid-Victorian calm was announced and enthusiastically acclaimed.'[1] Chartism and the other dangers of the 1840s were, if not overcome, at least contained. Britain had survived unscathed through the revolutionary years of 1848–49. Elsewhere the monarchies had on the whole been restored and where not, as most notably in France, the threats of anarchy and socialism seemed to have been overcome. For Britain the 'Great Exhibition' of 1851 signalled both its political and economic self-confidence. The 'Workshop of the World' was entering a period of global predominance almost certainly unequalled before or since. Mill, then, wrote *On Liberty* with its warning of decline at a time when British and European pre-eminence might well have appeared impregnable. Surely, it must have seemed, Britain had done everything right. So in 1859 Mill was, perhaps, anachronistically reiterating the pessimistic mood of the 1840s. As a self-proclaimed advanced thinker Mill might have responded with the view that he was ahead of his time rather than behind it. We can, if we want an alternative placing, regard Mill as having presciently shown awareness of Britain's loss of economic supremacy in the succeeding decades. Either way, Mill's mood was at variance with the dominant sentiment of the period in which *On Liberty* was published.

Like most authors, Mill's initial hopes for the book were very positive. Writing from Naples in 1855 – that is, when the essay was first being planned – Mill imagined that it would 'make a sensation'[2] and so it seemed to him it did, for one month after its publication in February 1859, he wrote to his friend Theodor Gomperz: 'The book has had much more success, and has made a greater impression, than I had the smallest expectation of.' In July Mill commented that the 'sale of so large an edition of the Liberty in so few months is very satisfactory'[3] and presumably it was, for a second edition appeared in August. This, on some accounts, was the prelude to a period of remarkable intellectual dominance. After Mill's death in 1873 the philosopher Henry Sidgwick reckoned that 'from about 1860–65 or thereabouts he ruled England in the region of thought as very few men ever did'.[4] Sidgwick's cut-off point of 1865 was the year in which Mill became Liberal MP for Westminster. In the following few years Mill undermined his credibility through his appeal for votes for women in 1867 and the publication of *Subjection of Women* in 1869. Looking back from the beginning of the twentieth century the jurist A. V. Dicey added another five years to those of Sidgwick, declaring that Mill was 'at the height of his power' between 1860 and 1870. At that time his 'authority among the educated youth of England was greater than may appear credible to the present generation. His work *On Liberty* was to the younger body of Liberal statesmen a political manual.'[5] Peter Nicholson, writing in 1998, gave Mill twenty years of dominance. 'Mill's reputation was', he says, 'at its height in the 1850s and 1860s, particularly at the universities, where his views were adopted by many of the next generation of political leaders and formers of opinion.' Nicholson then reduced the adulation by correctly noting that the 'impact of his political writings was more patchy; sometimes well received by political radicals, they were highly unpopular in many quarters'.[6] Janice Carlisle quite wrongly states that *On Liberty* was recognized by Mill's 'contemporaries as the "gospel" of the nineteenth century'. She notes 'Mill's contempt for his contemporaries'[7] but not that some of them, particularly the more conservative and religious, didn't think too much of him either.

What was also quite common in the early reviews was praise for the philosopher but dissent from his opinions. Henry Thomas Buckle regarded Mill as 'one of the most daring and original philosophers in Europe'. Buckle was the author of a highly influential, but uncompleted, *History of Civilization*, the first part of which had been published in 1857. His review of *On Liberty* in *Fraser's Magazine* of May 1859 began as follows: 'If a jury of the greatest European thinkers were to ... declare by their verdict whom among our living writers, had done most for the advance of knowledge, they could hardly hesitate in pronouncing the name of John Stuart Mill.'[8] Although

Buckle agreed on the need for greater liberty of discussion, he rejected fears that progress was coming to a halt, denied that liberty was in danger and did not feel that individuality was diminishing.

Another review of the same year was by Richard Holt Hutton in the unitarian journal *National Review*. Here we have an even starker example of praise for the man but dissent from his opinions. Hutton described Mill as a 'writer who has perhaps exercised more influence over the formation of the philosophical and social principles of cultivated Englishmen than any other man of his generation'. Yet many English reviewers found it hard to credit *On Liberty* as applying to their own country. They suggested that Mill's message was actually most needed in Spain, Italy, Portugal and Russia. Hutton felt that Mill adopted the tone of a dissident imprisoned by a despotic government. *On Liberty*, he thought, 'might almost, indeed, have come from the prison-cell of some persecuted thinker bent on making one last protest against the growing tyranny of the public mind'. Even worse, Mill was 'totally wrong in the most important of his preliminary assumptions'.[9]

On our main issue of the dangers of conformity and stagnation, Mill's contemporaries only occasionally alluded to it and then rarely took it seriously. John Rees has pointed out that the 'majority of those who discussed the essay during his lifetime were either decidedly against him or strangely silent on an issue which he took to be so fundamental'.[10] An anonymous reviewer in *British Quarterly Review* of 1860 did not see the dull and monochrome conformity of which Mill complained. 'On the contrary … never, since the world began, so far as history informs us, has there been an epoch distinguished by a greater *flush* of all sorts of opinions even the most reckless and absurd.' He then categorized the 'speculative monstrosities' enjoying unparalleled freedom. 'From the extremes of Communism to Despotism, from the extremes of Atheism and Pantheism to Mormonism', there is 'no folly of pseudo-philosophy, from Table-turning and Spirit-rapping to Biology and Clairvoyance, that has not graced our era.' Some eccentricities were harmless but, as a few critics pointed out, others were not. John Wilson, writing in the conservative *Quarterly Review* of 1873, feared that Mill's call for eccentricity would merely encourage toleration of views that were politically dangerous. 'In these days of the International, the Commune, Spanish and Irish Federalism, lack of eccentricity, at least in politics, is not perhaps the malady with which the World, whether Old or New, feels itself most afflicted.'[11]

Mill's foremost contemporary critic was the lawyer James Fitzjames Stephen, whose *Liberty, Equality, Fraternity* first appeared in the *Pall Mall Gazette* between November 1872 and January 1873 and in full book form in March 1873, just weeks before Mill's death on 7 May. Stephen, though a utilitarian, might be described as more authoritarian than liberal. For him it was force rather than discussion that determined how decisions were reached and so defending freedom of opinion was simply irrelevant as a means of achieving progress. Stephen mentioned 'Chinese uniformity' and wrote a bit on mass society, but soon moved to other issues because he saw no evidence of widespread conformity or similarity.

> I should certainly not agree with Mr. Mill's opinion that English people in general are dull, deficient in originality, and as like each other as herrings in a barrel appear to us. Many and many a fisherman, common sailor, workman, labourer, gamekeeper, policeman, non-commissioned officer, servant, and small clerk have I known who were just as distinct from each other, just as original in their own way, just as full of character, as men in a higher rank in life.[12]

Clearly the whole notion of the better few being engulfed by the mass, let alone of that process endangering civilization, made no impact on Stephen at all. He was far more concerned with the idea of utilitarianism as a substitute religion and with the indifference to Christianity that it implied. Otherwise, Stephen's lack of comment, favourable or otherwise, on Eastern stagnation is surprising because, like Mill, he also had Indian connections, having served there as Legal Member of the Viceroy's Council, and so might have had some thoughts on comparative civilizations. Furthermore, given the general tone of his attack, he seems unlikely to have deliberately neglected a chance to indicate where Mill had gone wrong.

In discussing *On Liberty*, Mill's close friend Alexander Bain thought that he 'too closely identifies energy with originality or genius, and genius with eccentricity. In regard to all these characteristics, many fine distinctions need to be drawn, over and above what Mill gives us.' Bain also failed to see in Mill's reference to 'the unprogressiveness of the East to the despotism of custom a wholly satisfactory explanation: the problem of stationary societies is still undecided'.[13]

Bain, then, at least referred to our topic. This was more than could be said for most critics of *On Liberty*. For them the claim that civilization was in danger was not only not taken seriously, it was rarely even discussed. This was because its postulate, conformity and the stultification of opinion, seemed quite unfounded at the time. As just one example, the *British Quarterly Review* declared that 'Never has there been a period in which men have either given expression to a greater number of speculative monstrosities, or avowed them with greater freedom or more enviable superiority to modesty and shame.'[14]

It is clear that what most upset Mill's contemporaries were his views on religion and women, and consequently the family. Possibly the notion that Western superiority was being eroded by mass society was ignored because it was too implausible. Yet this is how most of Mill's contemporaries regarded his views on women – and they certainly did not ignore *them*. Rather they thoroughly exposed, discussed and combated such threatening views. Here, ironically, Mill's critics confirmed the view that they had otherwise denied, for the negative reception given to Mill's *On the Subjection of Women* confirmed his own point that society had limited tolerance of divergent opinions.[15] Perhaps Mill's feminism had to be countered because it seemed to constitute incitement in a way that the mass society warning did not.

THE LATE-TWENTIETH-CENTURY FOCUS

Recent discussion of John Stuart Mill's *On Liberty* has focused on Mill's philosophy of the individual; of how he tried to find a principle of societal and political non-interference with individual opinion, and of whether this principle can be aligned with his declared utilitarianism. This has gone along with a relative neglect of his sociology of society. This is partially a consequence of the main academic location of Mill studies in philosophy departments and political philosophy courses in politics departments. Furthermore, sociology departments have moved more towards cultural studies and away from the classic thinkers of the nineteenth century from whom their discipline derives. Most recent analyses of Mill on the decline of individuality fail even to mention that for him this was simultaneously a threat to social improvement. To take just one example, John Robson has a chapter on 'Civilization and Culture as Moral Concepts' in *The Cambridge Companion to Mill*.[16] This is a volume that constitutes a thorough overview of Mill's thought and is likely to remain of fundamental importance for students into the foreseeable future. Robson made no mention at all of Mill's belief that Western civilization was in danger. John Gray also does not develop the full argument of how the threat to individuality endangers social progress. In *Mill On Liberty: A Defence*, Gray presents liberty almost entirely in terms of self-development, stating that 'Mill's doctrine of liberty postulates connections between liberty, self-development and happiness.'[17] There is no discussion of liberty as the means of social progress. Geraint Williams has made the standard point that '*On Liberty* was written in response to Mill's fear that ... individuality was under severe threat.'[18] This, on my argument, is obviously only half the point.

Moving to slightly less recent scholarship, we may note that Isaiah Berlin's famous article on 'John Stuart Mill and the Ends of Life' has nothing on society being endangered.[19] H. O. Pappé's 1964 article on 'Mill and Tocqueville', a plausible source for a discussion similar to ours, made no mention of mass society.[20] Pappé sought to downplay the influence granted to Tocqueville in I. W. Mueller's *John Stuart Mill and French Thought*,[21] which itself, neither in the chapter on 'The Influence of Alexis de Tocqueville' nor in the one that covers *On Liberty*, has anything significant on mass society and the threat of stagnation. Mueller's Chapter Five on 'The Influence of

Alexis de Tocqueville' deals mainly with the 1830s and 1840s, that is with Mill's reviews of *Democracy in America*, and so has nothing on the notion of civilization coming to a halt. Chapter Seven on 'The Later Years', that is those after 1848, has nothing on mass society, nor on Chinese stagnation. Alan Ryan's *J. S. Mill*, in the chapter on '*Liberty* and *The Subjection of Women*', made no mention of Mill's view that European pre-eminence was endangered.[22]

Gertrude Himmelfarb devoted a chapter of her book *On Liberty and Liberalism* to each chapter of *On Liberty*. Thus her Chapter Three is on Mill's Chapter Three, which she says 'may well be regarded as the heart of *On Liberty*', yet she did not mention Mill's belief that society faced stagnation. She speaks of where '*On Liberty* differed so markedly from most of Mill's other writings' and finds the 'other' Mill, not the one of *On Liberty*, more truly liberal; more in the heritage of Montesquieu, Burke, Tocqueville, and, later, Halévy, for whom liberty is not an absolute but one value that has to co-exist with others. Himmelfarb blames the alleged faults and simplicities of *On Liberty* on Mill's wife[23] and so concurs with his statement that the book was more decidedly hers than anything else he wrote,[24] although how much it was hers still remains a matter of debate.

Thus recent commentary shows less concern with Mill's most basic charge against his own society than with other important but ultimately less serious issues in his work. These other aspects, they might argue, were dealt with in a more satisfactory way by Mill and are thus greater contributions to knowledge and so more deserving of our attention. We have no argument against this case. Our assertion is merely that if Mill is to be taken as seriously as recent scholarship suggests, then, to reiterate, his major charge against his own society deserves to be given more attention than has previously been the case.

MILL AND LIBERALISM

In the six previous chapters we cut a path through some of the many issues on which Mill commented. It has not been the usual path but it was, it is hoped, an interesting and worthwhile one. In this concluding section we shall consider whether the perspective we gained modifies the dominant view of Mill's place at the head of British liberalism. In the 1920s R. H. Tawney described Mill as 'the last and the greatest of Liberal thinkers'.[25] Isaiah Berlin once described Mill as the man who 'founded modern liberalism' and *On Liberty* as 'the classic statement of the case for individual liberty'.[26] In the 1980s Anthony Arblaster referred to Mill as 'this central figure in modern liberalism'. He declared that in 'the English-speaking world no name is more habitually linked to that of liberalism than Mill's, and no single liberal text is better known than *On Liberty*'.[27] Lastly, John Gray, from whom more will be heard, has described Mill as 'in many respects *the* paradigm liberal thinker'.[28] This is all, presumably, fairly conclusive. A distinguished body of opinion over the last century places Mill at the forefront of liberal thinking. The components of his thought that give him that position are not hard to delineate. We can specify his opposition to the aristocracy, mass society and conformity as also his belief in individuality, freedom of thought, education, rationality, *laissez-faire* economics, representative government and equality for women. He was also, of course, a Liberal Member of Parliament for a few years.

However readers will by now realize that the situation is not so straightforward, for there are commentaries that seek either to deny or at least to modify Mill's identification with liberalism. The best-known attack on Mill's liberal credentials is Maurice Cowling's *Mill and Liberalism*, first published in 1963. Cowling boldly set out his position right from the start. In the Introduction he declared that he found in Mill 'more than a touch of something resembling moral totalitarianism'.[29] The attack continued with the statement that Mill's 'liberalism was neither comprehensive nor libertarian: it attempted dogmatically to erode the assumptions on which competing doctrines were based'. Cowling saw Mill as replacing the traditional authority of the Church and aristocracy with a new authority, that of the intellectual clerisy. This new authority would not necessarily be more liberal, libertarian or tolerant than the old one. It would merely be the replacement of one ruling class by another. Cowling then, in the year of the Cuba missile crisis, at the height of the Cold War, at a time when Western liberalism was generally seen as the ideology of freedom in global conflict with the ideology of Marxist totalitarianism, saw them as having similar negative features. Furthermore, in a link with the then current literature on totalitarianism and the 'authoritarian personality', these features were identified with the character of Mill himself. Thus Cowling declared that 'Liberalism, no less than Marxism, is intolerant of competition: jealousy, and a carefully disguised intolerance, are important features of Mill's intellectual personality.'[30]

More recently and more moderately, Joseph Hamburger has sought to modify the usual understanding of Mill's liberalism by asserting that several of its key features apply only in certain situations. Thus Hamburger upgraded the 1831 'Spirit of the Age' articles, particularly the Saint-Simonian idea of history having critical and organic periods. Placing this frame over *On Liberty* leads to the suggestion that the eccentric individual there recommended is appropriate *only* to the critical period of history when the work of destruction has to be done. What most commentary takes as timeless recommendations were seen by Hamburger as specifically related to just one part of the historical cycle. This, of course, makes Mill less the archetypal defender of liberty than is usually supposed.

Hamburger also upgraded the 'Bentham' and 'Coleridge' essays as the permanent models of Mill's project. On this understanding Bentham did the negative work and so was a thinker for the critical period when outmoded mores had to be undermined. Coleridge, in contrast, suggested what was needed for an organic phase: order, consensus and common values. In recommending the significance of both, Hamburger saw Mill, again, as compromising liberalism. Hamburger's title *Mill on Liberty and Control*,[31] as with the Bentham/Coleridge balance, further suggests the limits to Mill's liberalism. The less than fully liberal aspects of *On Liberty* and other writings are said to have been overlooked or relegated because many late-twentieth century liberals looked to Mill to provide a foundation statement of their own rather different views. Hamburger noted that 'Mill – especially the Mill of *On Liberty* – has always been linked to liberalism' but concluded that Mill's 'commitment to liberal values was diminished by another, not obviously compatible belief in the need to subdue and control the inherent selfishness of human nature by imposing order and authority upon it'.[32]

We shall, then, outline a number of areas where Mill diverges from the usual over-simple images of liberalism. The supposed illiberalism of empire will consequently be seen to be co-ordinate with other parts of Mill's thinking. If we start with liberty itself, for that is what Mill is pre-eminently seen as advocating, we have already noticed passages which seem to adopt a rather instrumental approach to it. In Chapter Two of *On Liberty* Mill referred to the 'principal causes which make diversity of opinion advantageous and will continue to do so until mankind shall have entered a stage of intellectual advancement which at present seems at an incalculable distance'. The 'until' seems to make freedom contingent upon society's particular stage of progress. Moving beyond that stage might still be 'an incalculable distance' away, but Mill's manner of stating the case does not seem to be that of someone for whom the preservation of liberty was an absolute principle. Nor was this an isolated aberration, for ten pages later Mill declared it 'useful that while mankind are imperfect there should be different opinions, so it is that there should be different experiments in living'.[33] On a plausible reading of this passage one could take 'different opinions' as means towards perfection rather than as values in themselves. On this logic, once, or if, perfection were reached, 'different opinions' would become redundant.

John Day has pointed out the result of Mill subsuming liberty within utilitarianism:

> One of the consequences of Mill's founding his principles of liberty solely on utilitarian criteria is that his case for liberty falls away if it can be demonstrated that liberty does not produce the benefits he claims for it. Since he does not value liberty for itself, but only for its consequences, he would be obliged to disown liberty when it did not tend to have the effects that he expected.

Day continues by pointing out that for Mill, 'The right to liberty is conditional, there is no abstract right to it. Although Mill is generally regarded as the apostle of liberalism, his support for liberty is significantly weaker than that of Locke who asserts that a human being has an unqualified right to liberty by virtue of his humanity.'[34] Liberalism is, among many other things, a theory of equal opportunity. It thus challenged the entrenched, traditional powers of aristocratic regimes. In the generation before Mill both Paine and Bentham, in their very different ways, had launched an onslaught against the sufficiency of precedent as a norm for social and political practices. Where Mill fits into the liberal camp is in his clear opposition to aristocratic power. This is clearly evident in his approach to its very core, landed property. However, we shall see that Mill's anti-aristocratic stance did not require that entailed land be fully subject to the unalloyed blast of the market; rather land transfers were to be modified in accord with notions of social responsibility under the directing hand of the state.

Mill had accepted Coleridge's arguments that, first, land had not actually been created by those who claimed ownership of it, and, second, that it should never be considered in isolation from the fate of those who lived and worked upon it. Land, consequently, should not be traded as if the only relevant consideration were its pecuniary reward. In applying this point to Ireland Mill declared it was unacceptable for a landowner to have the right to turn labourers 'out by hundreds and make them perish on the high road, as had been done before now by Irish landlords'. He thought that 'a mode of property in land which has brought things to this pass, has existed long enough'.[35] Mill learnt from his friend and India House colleague William Thornton that over six millions acres of Irish land were lying waste, well over half of which were suitable for agricultural purposes. There was, then, clearly sufficient and adequate land available for distribution to the peasants. It was, however, not actually in the public domain as commons but was rather the considerable unused territory of the large landowners. For Mill this was scarcely a disadvantage. There were circumstances in which the state had a duty to impinge on property rights. Mill proposed compulsory purchase of unused land, redistributing it to peasant families and granting adequate compensation to the former owners. One critic accused Mill of 'the doctrine of general spoliation … that a general confiscation of the landed property of a whole country shall take place'. Mill retorted that he proposed nothing beyond what had already occurred for the construction of canals, railways or turnpike roads. Thus he reduced the shock by stating that his means were already current practice. The rights of private property could legitimately be overridden when clear public needs were involved. 'Rights of property are conferred to promote the public good, not that they may be used as obstacles to it.' His message to the landowners was that 'we are going to take the land from you; to enter it, and do as we please with it, for the purpose of rendering it productive, whether with your leave or without it'.[36] As for the accusation of spoliation, it could not be sustained when compensation was paid.

Mill thus summoned the state to superintend the use of land by the owners of it. His assumption was that the state could be held responsible for its acts of omission as well as those of commission. The rights of private property could properly be overridden by the duties of social responsibility. Land owned beyond the extent required for family subsistence confers 'power over other human beings – power affecting them in their most vital interests'. If the state allows such a situation to occur it is thereby required to see 'that the power which it has so given shall not be abused'. It must, says Mill in a vital passage, use 'the full extent of its power' for ensuring the most productive use of the land, and the 'happiest existence'[37] to the greatest number that can be employed on it. Social utilitarianism, the greatest happiness of the greatest number, as decided by their representatives, here triumphs over individual utilitarianism, the right of each landowner to pursue his own happiness as he thinks best. The most prestigious property, that of land held in quantities beyond the plausible needs of a single family, as it so generally was, was to be confined within the bounds of social obligations.

If we move more directly to the central economic aspects of liberalism, we find that Mill was no unalloyed advocate of *laissez-faire*. He acknowledged the failings of capitalism and criticized the narrowness and selfishness of the commercial outlook. In his *Political Economy* he explained that the motive of ornamentation and fine clothes was a useful device for inducting 'a savage' into the habit of regular work, but added that in societies such as his own 'its indulgence tends to impoverish rather than to enrich' and that every 'real improvement in the character of the English ... must necessarily moderate the ardour of their devotion to the pursuit of wealth'.[38]

In his review of Tocqueville's second volume Mill pointed out that, even more than the schools, the place of employment served as a source of education. This, however, was a mixed blessing. For most workers the daily task was narrow and mechanical. It 'brings but few of his faculties into action'. Furthermore its 'exclusive pursuit' made the worker 'indifferent to the public, to the more generous objects and the nobler interests, and, in his inordinate regard for his personal comforts, selfish and cowardly'.[39] Even within formal education the pressure of commercial values made itself felt. Mill complained that 'hardly any branch of education is valued, hardly any kind of knowledge cultivated, which does not lead in the directest way to some money-getting end'.[40] Although he favoured commerce, Mill still wanted it kept within bounds. Accumulation should not be allowed to stifle cultivation. Mill concluded that the 'most serious danger to the future prospects of mankind is in the unbalanced influence of the commercial spirit'.[41] He hoped that in time the competitive and acquisitive stage of human development would come to an end. People would acknowledge that there was more to life than material success. Mill declared himself

Not charmed with the ideal of life held out by those who think that the normal state of human beings is that of struggling to get on; that the trampling, crushing, elbowing, and treading on each other's heads, which form the existing type of social life, are the most desirable lot of human kind, or anything but the disagreeable symptoms of one of the phases of industrial progress.[42]

This situation would be replaced by the stationary state, a term that has been widely misunderstood and quite wrongly associated with Chinese stagnation. We have already noted that the stationary state was one in which only the level of capital and population would be at a standstill. It was, then, *not* the end of development as such but only the termination of the economic forms necessary to raise productivity. Other developments would continue. Mill's standpoint, then, was clearly less that of the business sector than of the educated and cultivated professional middle class, a group with an ethic of service to society as a whole. On this basis Mill attempted, however unsuccessfully, to push the individualist utilitarian ethic of his father and Bentham more directly towards a concern for society as a whole. The calculating individual was now asked not merely to estimate personal advantage but also to consider the general good.

In terms of the conventional categories this standpoint did not so much distance Mill from liberalism as specify his place within it. His writings mark a transition between the so-called classical liberal political economy of Adam Smith and David Ricardo and the 'new liberalism' associated first with T. H. Green and then with J. A. Hobson and L. T. Hobhouse.[43] The difference between the two liberalisms is nowhere more marked than in its attitude to *laissez-faire* and the role of the state. Mill clearly marked out his position astride the two liberalisms when declaring that *laissez-faire*, 'the practical principle of non-interference', was 'unquestionably sound as a general rule; but there is no difficulty in perceiving some very large and conspicuous exceptions to it'.[44] To understand one category of such exceptions we must turn to a key question for the understanding of Mill's philosophy: the functions and limits of state action.

Mill was in principle suspicious of the state. It already had too much power and too extensive an influence. Officials, even of a liberal and constitutional state, could be just as tyrannical as those of a despotism. People understand their own business better than the government does, and most things are done worse by government than they would be by 'the individuals most interested in the matter'.[45] Furthermore, and crucially, the greater the extent of governmental activity, the smaller the area remaining for individual exertion and self-improvement. Such individual activity should have both its proper scope and its own rewards. Thus Mill opposed a progressive income tax. Such a measure would 'impose a penalty on people for having worked harder and saved more than their neighbours'.[46]

131

Mill shared, indeed exemplified, the liberal attempt to protect individuality by erecting barriers around it. Mill's attempt to establish a distinction between self- and other-regarding actions is, perhaps, the most famous example. This was no simple issue, however, for society had 'no recognised principle by which the propriety or impropriety of government interference is customarily tested'.[47] In *Political Economy* Mill conceded the impossibility of producing 'the ring-fence of any restrictive definition'[48] within which the functions of government could be confined. He also admitted 'the necessary functions of government' to be 'considerably more multifarious than most people are at first aware of, and not capable of being circumscribed by those very definite lines of demarcation, which, in the inconsiderateness of popular discussion, it is often attempted to draw round them'.[49] The repetition is just one indication that Mill was arguing less with the reader than with himself. He would dearly have liked a principle by which the state could be kept at bay. The Englishman's home is his castle and Mill was vainly attempting to hold the fort. He had hardly begun, however, before he had to admit concessions. Principles are what he hoped to apply but, outside of his more theoretical chapters, he finds that they continuously retreat before expediency. As he delves more precisely into his problem we find that the areas of legitimate state action seem to grow while his examples of improper state interference remain few. W. H. Greenleaf, watching carefully for such developments, notes that 'Mill goes in principle quite a way on the collectivist road'.[50]

For the anarchist there are no hard decisions on when to curb the state, for it is to be reduced completely. For Mill, however, suspicious of the state but committed to personal self-development, the latter comes to require the former. The context that an individual and a society need in which to prosper demands, just for a start, an infrastructure of order, a legal system, standard weights and measures, roads and canals.

Thus far we are possibly still within the confines of the so-called 'minimal state'. It is less obvious that we remain so when Mill acknowledges that emerging industries may need protection, that the supply of currency should be controlled by the state, and that the mentally ill must be cared for. Mill also noted that nobody seemed to object when the state builds lighthouses or makes harbours, dykes and embankments. He accepted that gas and water belonged to the category of natural monopolies and that these, like the paving and cleaning of the streets, were best arranged by the municipal authorities and paid for out of the rates. In respect of roads, canals and railways, Mill thought that though voluntary associations might rent and run them, they should be strictly controlled by the government, which could hold the right to fix fares and charges or even 'reserve to itself a reversionary property in such public works'.[51]

Mill's views on female subordination have received much attention, initially in order to ridicule him, but since the advent of second-wave feminism in the 1960s, to hail him as a pioneer of the movement. Less attention has been given to his case for the state to have a controlling influence on marriage and the family. This was an area where our advocate of liberty thought that current liberties should be withheld. Turning first to marriage itself, Mill declared it no infringement of liberty for the state to forbid the right of marriage to couples unable to support a family financially. This was, evidently, the situation in 'many countries', unnamed, 'on the Continent'.[52] On this notion the state could legitimately impose a financial qualification for marriage, decide the level of that qualification and so veto those applicants who fail to meet it. This harsh proposal is a consequence of Mill's Malthusian fear of over-population and is part of the mindset that led him to support the notorious 1834 Poor Law Amendment Act which, among other things, separated husbands from wives in the workhouses that it established. We have here the paradox that the liberal ideal of individual responsibility requires the state to police those unable to achieve its requirements.

The next step after marriage was parenthood. Here Mill was suspicious. 'Parental power', he warned, 'is as susceptible of abuse as any other power, and is, as a matter of fact, constantly abused'.[53] Parents were the nominal protectors of their children, yet Mill recognized that the latter may need protection from them. Thus our opponent of the paternal state has to allow it a literally paternalistic role, for where necessary it has to institute a good that many parents failed to supply. From Mill's viewpoint, an important part of providing for a family consisted in paying for the education of the children. At a time when conservatives were worried that the children of the poor might get educated beyond their station, liberals, in the best Enlightenment tradition, saw education as a means of both personal and social development. It was, perhaps, the key ingredient of social progress. Failure to provide a child with not only 'food for its body' but also 'instruction and training for its mind, is a moral crime' which the state ought to remedy. Mill was distinctly uneasy about state education, which would be 'a mere contrivance for moulding people to be exactly like one another', precisely the situation that *On Liberty* was written to counteract. In that work he explicitly objected to a situation in which the state provided 'a whole or any large part of the education of the people'.[54] A decade earlier, however, in *Political Economy*, he had classified education as one of many 'things which are chiefly useful as tending to raise the character of human beings' yet in which the market demonstrated its incapacity. It responded to wants rather than needs and so, to redress its limitations, education becomes 'one of those things which it is admissible in principle that a government should provide for the people'.[55] Clearly the principles of *On Liberty* would not be undermined by a state which provided only a small part of the society's schooling. However, his actual proposal in *On Liberty* was not the same as that in *Political Economy*, for now the government does no more than provide the funding for poor parents to purchase their children's education from independent providers, a scheme now associated with the idea of education vouchers. Even here, however, if one thinks about the problems of implementation, it is not clear that Mill has held the state at bay to the extent he assumed. It is hard to see how the demand for universal education can be combined with limited state control, for clearly the provision of even universal elementary education, at that or any other time, would have been possible only with the state as the paymaster, if not the provider, but still thereby having the overwhelmingly dominant influence.

After marrying, having children and paying for their education, the literally last thing parents can do for them is leave them their wealth. In most cases there was no wealth to leave, so the issue did not arise. Where there was, surely parents were showing their sense of responsibility by their final act of support? For Mill, however, it was not that simple. Just as it was an offence to provide too little for one's children, so also was it unacceptable to provide too much. This scenario brings us back once again to the aristocracy. As an advocate of radical improvements, Mill was frustrated by the extent to which British law fortified the survival of aristocratic advantage. Primogeniture gave fortunes to eldest sons who had done nothing to deserve them and thus stood in the path of economic development.

Mill's proposal was to limit the amount that anyone could receive by inheritance or bequest. He associated the *principle* of private property with exertion in the context of market insecurities and found it unacceptable to allow anyone to be placed above these exigencies. He proposed a maximum that an individual could inherit that would be at a level no higher than 'the means of comfortable independence'.[56] The implication of the controls on land ownership and on bequest is surely enhanced state activity. Judgement would have to be made on land usage, wills would have to be scrutinized, and expert evaluations ascertaining the precise current level of 'comfortable independence' would have to be continually updated.

The state, then, is either prohibitive or facilitative. The boundary of its activities cannot be wholly determined by a principle about its own intrinsic scope but rather also by a decision as to whether it serves to augment or retard personal and societal development in particular instances. Mill's instinct was to present state interference as an unusual breach of a norm and in need of special justification, but gradually the exceptions seem to become less exceptional.

We must now take a last look at Mill's treatment of imperialism. We mentioned in the fourth part of Chapter 3 that Mill allowed the state much more scope in a backward society than in a developed one, so in relation to the former he was much less of a classical liberal. Colonized societies had the benefit of rule of law, but not of self-government or the limited state. Mill's utilitarian branch of liberalism did not believe in human rights anyway, but clearly 'barbarian' peoples were not even granted the utilitarian provision of freedom to define and seek happiness in their own way. We have discussed Mill's view that freedom is appropriate for people only at a certain stage of their development. This approach adopts towards people judged as less mature the very paternalism that it explicitly rejects in terms of welfare and the economy. For Uday Mehta the 'irony of liberal defence of empire' is that its 'defence vitiates what we take liberalism to represent and historically stand for'.[57] If one thinks not just of John Stuart Mill but also of James Mill and Palmerston, however, Mehta makes it clear that in the nineteenth century liberalism and imperialism were not necessarily antithetical. Among Mill's liberal contemporaries there were varying attitudes to imperialism.[58] As examples of a rather different approach from Mill's, we can instance the cases of Lord Macaulay and John Bright.

Lord Macaulay was an MP intermittently between 1830 and 1856. In his book on *The English Utilitarians and India* Eric Stokes refers to him as the 'most representative figure' of English liberalism 'in both England and in India'.[59] In 1833, just a year before he became legal adviser to the supreme Council of India, Macaulay had informed Parliament: 'We are free, we are civilized, to little purpose, if we grudge to any portion of the human race an equal measure of freedom and civilization.' He thought that once the Indians were educated and knowledgeable they might, 'in some future age, demand European institutions. Whether such a day will ever come I know not. But never will I attempt to avert or retard it. Whenever it comes, it will be the proudest day in English history.'[60] Macaulay wanted the Indians to become more like the English and so showed little regard for Indian culture, yet he came a lot nearer than Mill to both envisaging and welcoming the possibility of Indian independence.

John Bright was a Liberal Member of Parliament from 1843 to 1889. He was not anti-imperialist in the sense of wanting all the colonies to be given full independence but he, nevertheless, struck what we would certainly now recognize as a more liberal tone in respect of it. He was thus in favour of British rule in India but critical of how it had been carried out. Taxes on the Indians were too high and the concern for their education too low. He called for tolerance of Indian religions and considered the British East India Company arrogant and tyrannical because it was not checked by public opinion. Where Mill defended the British presence on the paternal basis of achieving Indian development, Bright was quite clear that British plunder was the underlying cause. Just after the Indian Mutiny, at a time when British attention was focused on the horrors perpetrated by the other side, Bright chose to remind the House of Commons that 'We are in the position of invaders and conquerors – they are in the position of the invaded and conquered.'[61] The point was reiterated in a speech to his constituents in Birmingham: 'We seized a considerable kingdom in India ... we committed a

great immorality and a great crime, and we have reaped an almost instanta-
neous retribution in the most gigantic and sanguinary revolt which probably
any nation ever made against its conquerors.' In the same speech he adopted
a rather different tone on the first opium war from that of John Stuart Mill:
'No man', said Bright, 'with a spark of morality in his composition, no man
who cares anything for the opinion of his fellow-countrymen, has dared to
justify that war.'[62]

So, even though Mill's imperialism did not fully contradict his liberalism
we can certainly conclude that it made him less liberal than some of his
contemporaries. A linked problem area for liberal ideology has been its
association with government by consent. Early liberalism valued consent but
disavowed democracy. What they favoured was a government held responsible to those viewed as legitimate actors in politics: the landed and
professional classes and, on some estimates, the educated also. Consent in
liberalism was sometimes highlighted in principle but diminished in application. It is said that John Locke in particular blazed the liberal trail by
highlighting the principle of government by consent. For Locke, however, the
only consent worthy of the name occurs at the original institution of government. From that time on consent is merely 'tacit' as indicated by residence
within the territory. So early liberalism introduced a principle which may be
said, with the aid of hindsight, to have had democratic implications but was
certainly not immediately seen to require universal suffrage. The curtailment
of democracy occurred because government by consent was just one of a
number of principles with which liberalism was associated. Another, of particular relevance here, was rational government. Government could be rational
only if the electors were rational. Those deemed not to be so were, on that
liberal principle, which was one that Mill held, legitimately downgraded. For
this reason Mill proposed educational qualifications for the franchise and
weighted plural voting.[63] This contained the possibility that in time all adults
might qualify, but, from Mill's perspective, that prospect was not imminent.

To judge the issue of whether, or how far, Mill's imperialism and his reser-
vations on democracy qualify his liberalism depends upon how we define
liberalism itself. Unfortunately this is no easy matter. John Gray has dealt
with the relationship of Mill to liberalism as follows: 'If anyone has ever been
a true liberal, it was John Stuart Mill, but defining his liberalism is not easy,
for all that. There is no broad agreement among social philosophers as to the
defining features of liberalism, which we can use as a benchmark for Mill's
liberal commitment. On any sensible understanding, however, Mill is a
paradigmatic liberal.' Gray has also described *On Liberty* as 'Mill's most
liberal work'.[64] Alan Ryan similarly finds it 'clear beyond doubt' that *On
Liberty* 'is a liberal manifesto' and also finds it hard to be definite about liberalism itself. He continues: '*what* the liberalism is that it defends and *how* it
defends it remain matters of controversy'. He also finds Mill an 'awkward

ally of twentieth-century liberals'.[65] This point of disjunction between
nineteenth- and twentieth-century liberals does give us a lead in reducing,
though not resolving, the definitional difficulty. Thus, rather than the hopeless
endeavour of pursuing a timeless definition, we can adopt a more modest
stance and regard liberalism, or any other ideology, as a developing tradition
of thought whose features and focus have varied from one time and place to
another. Consequently we need not be troubled or embarrassed to discover
beliefs historically associated with liberalism that its more recent proponents
have found convenient to forget. This means that liberalism was once not
what it now is and so, in its historical totality, may not be quite what many
people think it is.

This study has highlighted some of the boundaries of consent theory in
nineteenth-century liberalism. It has thus explained Mill's belief that
backward societies were not yet fit for liberty or self-government. They were
not even granted the utilitarian provision of freedom to define and seek happiness in their own way. Mill's fuller liberalism was clearly for more advanced
societies. Even there it is not clear that Mill was straightforwardly democratic,
for he was more concerned to promote the influence of the best rather than of
the most. In terms of liberalism's various aspects we can agree with Isaiah
Berlin that desirable ends necessarily conflict, that one can't have everything
simultaneously and that for Mill the pursuit of rationality had priority over the
postulate of government by consent. On precisely that basis those he deemed
civilized could legitimately control those they judged to be barbarian.

NOTES

1. G. Best, *Mid-Victorian Britain 1851–1875* (Glasgow: Fontana, 1982), pp. 250, 253.
2. MCW, XIV, p. 332.
3. MCW, XV, pp. 613, 630.
4. Quoted in J. Skorupski (ed.), *The Cambridge Companion to Mill* (Cambridge: Cambridge University Press, 1998), p. 1.
5. A. V. Dicey, *Law and Opinion in England During the Nineteenth Century* [1905] (London: Macmillan, 1963), p. 386.
6. P. Nicholson, 'The Reception and Early Reputation of Mill's Political Thought', in J. Skorupski (ed.), *The Cambridge Companion to Mill*, p. 466.
7. J. Carlisle, *John Stuart Mill and the Writing of Character* (Athens, GA: University of Georgia Press, 1991), pp. xii, 13.
8. Quoted in A. Pyle (ed.), *Liberty: Contemporary Responses to John Stuart Mill* (Bristol: Thoemmes Press, 1994), pp. 26, 25.
9. Ibid., p. 81.
10. J. C. Rees, *Mill and His Early Critics* (Leicester: Leicester University Press, 1956), p. 9.

11. Pyle, *Liberty*, pp. 209, 326.
12. J. Fitzjames Stephen, *Liberty, Equality, Fraternity* [1873] (Indianapolis, IN: Liberty Fund, 1993), pp. 30, 158; see also pp. 20, 157.
13. A. Bain, *John Stuart Mill: A Criticism with Personal Recollections* [1882] (New York: A. M. Kelly, 1969), p. 107.
14. Pyle, *Liberty*, p. 209.
15. See Nicholson in Skorupski (ed.), *Cambridge Companion to Mill*, p. 471.
16. J. Skorupski (ed.) (Cambridge: Cambridge University Press, 1988), ch. 9.
17. J. Gray, *Mill on Liberty: A Defence*, 2nd edn (London: Routledge, 1996), p. 15; see also pp. 47, 142, 156. On p. 119 Gray refers to Mill's 'belief in the practical irreversibility of the condition of freedom', sensibly reversing that judgement one page later by acknowledging that for Mill 'we have no assurance that civilisation can always be maintained. Barbarism remains a permanent possibility.'
18. G. L. Williams, 'Changing Reputations and Interpretations in the History of Political Thought: J. S. Mill', *Politics*, 15 (3), September 1995, pp. 183–9, esp. p. 184.
19. In I. Berlin, *Four Essays on Liberty* (London: Oxford University Press, 1969).
20. H. O. Pappé, 'Mill and Tocqueville', *Journal of the History of Ideas*, 25, 1964, pp. 217–34.
21. I. W. Mueller, *John Stuart Mill and French Thought* (Urbana: University of Illinois Press, 1956).
22. A. Ryan, *J. S. Mill* (London: Routledge and Kegan Paul, 1974), ch. 5.
23. G. Himmelfarb, *On Liberty and Liberalism: The Case of John Stuart Mill* (New York: Knopf, 1974), p. 73; see also pp. 338, 257f.
24. Ibid., pp. 71, 73 and see pp. xi, xix, 168, 257f. It is interesting to note the extent to which Harriet Taylor's 1832 essay prefigures the theme of mass society and the threat to the individual. The essay is reprinted as Appendix II of F. von Hayek, *John Stuart Mill and Harriet Taylor* (London: Routledge, 1951), pp. 275–9.
25. R. H. Tawney, *The Acquisitive Society* [1921] (London: Bell, 1948), p. 102.
26. I. Berlin, 'John Stuart Mill and the Ends of Life', in *Four Essays on Liberty* (London: Oxford University Press, 1969), pp. 173, 174.
27. A. Arblaster, *The Rise and Decline of Western Liberalism* (Oxford: Blackwell, 1984), p. 277.
28. J. Gray, *Liberalism*, 2nd edn (Buckingham: Open University Press, 1995), p. 87.
29. M. Cowling, *Mill and Liberalism* (Cambridge: Cambridge University Press, 1963), p. xii.
30. Ibid., p. xiii. See also the review article 'Was Mill for Liberty?' by John Rees in *Political Studies*, XIV(1), February 1966, pp. 72–7. Further on alleged liberal illiberalism, Bhiku Parekh has written of a 'Millian commitment to a single mode of human excellence'. See 'Superior People: The Narrowness of Liberalism from Mill to Rawls', *The Times Literary Supplement*, 25 February 1994, p. 13.
31. J. Hamburger, *Mill on Liberty and Control* (Princeton, NJ: Princeton University Press, 2001).
32. Ibid., pp. 225, 234.
33. *On Liberty*, pp. 47, 57.
34. J. Day, 'John Stuart Mill: *On Liberty*', in M. Forsyth, M. Keens-Soper and J. Hoffman (eds), *The Political Classics: Hamilton to Mill* (Oxford: Oxford University Press, 1993), pp. 236, 237. See also J. Gray, 'Anti-liberal elements began to enter into the

liberal tradition itself from the mid-1840s in the work of John Stuart Mill', *Liberalism*, 2nd edn, p. 32.

35. MCW, X, p. 157.
36. MCW, XXIV, pp. 904, 921, 939.
37. MCW, X, p. 158.
38. MCW, II, pp. 104–5.
39. MCW, XVIII, p. 169.
40. MCW, XXII, p. 720.
41. MCW, XVIII, p. 198.
42. MCW, III, p. 754.
43. See W. H. Greenleaf, *The British Political Tradition*, vol. 2, *The Ideological Heritage* (London: Routledge, 1988), ch. 3.
44. MCW, III, p. 951.
45. Ibid., p. 941.
46. Ibid., p. 811.
47. *On Liberty*, p. 12.
48. MCW, III, p. 804.
49. Ibid., p. 800.
50. Greenleaf, *British Political Tradition*, vol. 2, p. 113.
51. MCW, III, p. 956.
52. *On Liberty*, p. 108.
53. MCW, III, p. 952.
54. *On Liberty*, pp. 105–6.
55. MCW, III, pp. 947–8.
56. MCW, II, p. 225.
57. U. Mehta, *Liberalism and Empire: A Study in Nineteenth-Century British Liberal Thought* (Chicago, IL: University of Chicago Press, 1999), pp. 3–4.
58. The same was true of German liberals. See Wolfgang J. Mommsen, 'Wandlungen der Liberalen Idee im Zeitalter des Imperialismus', in K. Holl and G. List (eds), *Liberalismus und Imperialistischer Staat* (Göttingen: Vandenhoeck and Ruprecht, 1975), esp. pp. 122–4.
59. E. Stokes, *The English Utilitarians and India* (Delhi: Oxford University Press, 1992), p. xiv.
60. Speech in the House of Commons, 10July 1833. Quoted in A. Bullock and M. Shock, *The Liberal Tradition: From Fox to Keynes* (London: A. and C. Black, 1956), p. 95.
61. *Speeches on Questions of Public Policy*, ed. James E. Thorold Rogers, 2 vols (London: Macmillan, 1869), vol. 1, p. 58.
62. Ibid., vol. 2, p. 384.
63. See MCW, XIX, pp. 324–5.
64. J. Gray, *Mill on Liberty: A Defence*, 2nd edn (London: Routledge, 1996), pp. 119, 57.
65. A. Ryan, 'Mill in a Liberal Landscape', in Skorupski (ed.), *Cambridge Companion to Mill*, pp. 497, 507.

Bibliography

1. J. S. MILL'S WRITINGS

Auguste Comte and Positivism (Ann Arbor, MI: University of Michigan Press, 1965).

Collected Works of John Stuart Mill, 33 vols, General Editor J. M. Robson (Toronto: University of Toronto Press, 1963–91).

Collini, S. (ed.) *J. S. Mill: On Liberty and Other Writings* (Cambridge: Cambridge University Press, 1989).

Haac, O. A. (ed.), *The Correspondence of John Stuart Mill and Auguste Comte* (New Brunswick, NJ, 1995).

Ryan, A. (ed.), *J. S. Mill and J. Bentham, Utilitarianism and Other Essays* (Harmondsworth: Penguin Books, 1987).

Utilitarianism, Liberty, Representative Government (London: Dent, 1962).

Williams, G. L. (ed.), *John Stuart Mill: On Politics and Society* (Hassocks: Harvester Press, 1976).

2. J. S. MILL: SECONDARY SOURCES

Bain, A., *John Stuart Mill. A Criticism with Personal Recollections* [1882] (New York: A. M. Kelley, 1969).

Baum, B., *Rereading Power and Freedom in J. S. Mill* (Toronto: Toronto University Press, 2000).

Berlin, I., 'John Stuart Mill and the Ends of Life', in *Four Essays on Liberty* (London: Oxford University Press, 1969).

Biagini, E. F., 'Liberalism and Direct Democracy: John Stuart Mill and the Model of Ancient Athens', in E. F. Biagini (ed.), *Citizenship and Community: Liberals, Radicals and Collective Identities in the British Isles, 1865–1931* (Cambridge: Cambridge University Press, 1996), ch. 1.

Canovan, M., 'The Eloquence of John Stuart Mill', *History of Political Thought*, VIII(3), Winter 1987, pp. 505–20.

Carlisle, J., *John Stuart Mill and the Writing of Character* (Athens, GA: University of Georgia Press, 1991).

Coleman, J., 'John Stuart Mill on the French Revolution', *History of Political Thought*, VI(1), Spring 1983, pp. 89–110.

Cowling, M., *Mill and Liberalism* (Cambridge: Cambridge University Press, 1963).

Day, J. 'John Stuart Mill: *On Liberty*', in M. Forsyth, M. Keens-Soper and J. Hoffman (eds), *The Political Classics: Hamilton to Mill* (Oxford: Oxford University Press, 1993), ch. 7.

Dicey, A. V., *Law and Opinion in England during the Nineteenth Century* [1905] (London: Macmillan, 1963).

Duncan, G., *Marx and Mill: Two Views of Social Conflict and Social Harmony* (Cambridge: Cambridge University Press, 1973).

Eisenach, E. J., 'Mill's *Autobiography* as Political Theory', *History of Political Thought*, VIII(1), Spring 1987, pp. 111–29.

Friedman, R., 'A New Exploration of Mill's Essay *On Liberty*', *Political Studies*, XIV(3), 1966, pp. 281–304.

Gray, J., *Mill on Liberty: A Defence* (London: Routledge, 1996).

Hamburger, J., *John Stuart Mill on Liberty and Control* (Princeton, NJ: Princeton University Press, 1999).

Hayek, F. A., *John Stuart Mill and Harriet Taylor: Their Friendship and Subsequent Marriage* (London: Routledge, 1951).

Himmelfarb, G., *On Liberty and Liberalism: The Case of John Stuart Mill* (New York: Knopf, 1974).

Kinzer, B., *England's Disgrace? J. S. Mill and the Irish Question* (Toronto: University of Toronto Press, 2001).

Kurfirst, R., 'J. S. Mill on Oriental Despotism, Including Its British Variant', *Utilitas*, 8(1), March 1996, pp. 73–87.

Levin, M., *The Condition of England Question: Carlyle, Mill, Engels* (Basingstoke: Macmillan, 1998).

——, 'On a Contradiction in Mill's Argument for Liberty', *Politics*, 19(3), September 1999, pp. 153–7.

——, 'John Stuart Mill: A Liberal Looks at Utopian Socialism in the Years of Revolution 1848–49', *Utopian Studies* (forthcoming).

Mazlish, B., *James and John Stuart Mill: Father and Son in the Nineteenth Century* (London: Hutchinson, 1975).

Moir, M. I., D. M. Peers, L. Zastoupil (eds), *J. S. Mill's Encounter with India* (Toronto: University of Toronto Press, 1999).

Mueller, I. W., *John Stuart Mill and French Thought* (Urbana, IL: University of Illinois Press, 1956).

Nicholson, P., 'The Reception and Early Reputation of Mill's Political Thought', in J. Skorupski (ed.), *The Cambridge Companion to Mill*.

Packe, M. St. J., *The Life of John Stuart Mill* (London: Secker and Warburg, 1954).

Pappé, H. O., 'Mill and Tocqueville', *Journal of the History of Ideas*, 25, 1964, pp. 217–34.

Parekh, B., 'Superior People: The Narrowness of Liberalism from Mill to Rawls', *Times Literary Supplement, 25* February 1994, pp. 11–13.

——, 'Liberalism and Colonialism: A Critique of Locke and Mill', in J. N. Pieterse and B. Parekh (eds), *The Decolonization of Imagination: Culture, Knowledge and Power* (Delhi: Oxford University Press, 1997).

Plamenatz, J. P., *The English Utilitarians* (Oxford: Blackwell, 1958).

Pyle, A. (ed.), *Liberty. Contemporary Responses to John Stuart Mill* (Bristol: Thoemmes Press, 1994).

Rees, J. C., *Mill and his Early Critics* (Leicester: Leicester University Press, 1956).

——, 'Was Mill for Liberty?', *Political Studies*, XIV(1), February 1966, pp. 72–7.

Robson, J. M., *The Improvement of Mankind: The Social and Political Thought of John Stuart Mill* (London: Routledge and Kegan Paul, 1968).

Ryan, A., 'Utilitarianism and Bureaucracy: The Views of J. S. Mill', in G. Sutherland (ed.), *Studies in the Growth of Nineteenth-Century Government* (London: Routledge and Kegan Paul, 1972).

——, *J. S. Mill* (London: Routledge and Kegan Paul, 1974).

——, 'Mill and Rousseau: Utility and Rights', in G. Duncan (ed.), *Democratic Theory and Practice* (Cambridge: Cambridge University Press, 1983).

——, 'Mill in a Liberal Landscape', in J. Skorupski (ed.), *The Cambridge Companion to Mill*.

Skorupski, J., (ed.), *The Cambridge Companion to Mill* (Cambridge: Cambridge University Press, 1998).

Stafford, W., *John Stuart Mill* (Basingstoke: Macmillan, 1998).

Stephen, J. Fitzjames, *Liberty, Equality, Fraternity* [1873] (Indianapolis, IN: Liberty Fund, 1993).

Sullivan, E. P., 'Liberalism and Imperialism: J. S. Mill's Defense of the British Empire', *Journal of the History of Ideas*, 44(4), 1983, pp. 599–617.

Thomas, W., *Mill* (Oxford: Oxford University Press, 1985).

Varouxakis, G., 'John Stuart Mill on Race', *Utilitas*, 10(1), March 1998, pp. 17–32.

——, 'Guizot's Historical Works and J. S. Mill's Reception of Tocqueville', *History of Political Thought*, XX(2), Summer 1999, pp. 292–312.

——, *Mill on Nationality* (London: Routledge, 2002).

Williams, G. L., 'Changing Reputations and Interpretations in the History of Political Thought: J. S. Mill', *Politics*, 15(3), September 1995, pp. 183–9.

Zastoupil, L., *John Stuart Mill and India* (Stanford, CA: Stanford University Press, 1994).

3. OTHER WORKS USED

Annual Register 1859 (London: Longman, 1860).
Arblaster, A., *The Rise and Decline of Western Liberalism* (Oxford: Blackwell, 1984).
Bagehot, W., *Physics and Politics* [1872] (London: Kegan Paul, n.d.).
Bain, A. *James Mill: A Biography* [1882] (New York: A. M. Kelley, 1967).
Bearce, G. D., *British Attitudes Towards India 1784–1858* (Oxford, Oxford University Press, 1961).
Belchem, J., *Popular Radicalism in Nineteenth-Century Britain* (Basingstoke: Macmillan, 1996).
Bentham, J., 'Essay on the Influence of Time and Place in Matters of Legislation' [1782] in J. Bowring (ed.), *The Works of Jeremy Bentham*, Part 1 (Edinburgh: Tait, 1838).
——, *The Theory of Legislation* [1802] (London: Kegan Paul, 1931).
——, *The Principles of Morals and Legislation* [1789] (New York: Hafner, 1965).
——, 'Emancipate Your Colonies! Address to the National Convention of France, 1793, Shewing the Uselessness and Mischievousness of Distant Dependencies to an European State', in *The Collected Works of Jeremy Bentham: Rights, Representation, and Reform. Nonsense Upon Stilts and Other Writings on the French Revolution* ed. P. Shofield, C. Pease Watkin and C. Blamires (Oxford: Clarendon Press, 2002).
Berlin, I., *The First and the Last* (London: Granta Books, 1999).
Berry, C., *Social Theory of the Scottish Enlightenment* (Edinburgh: Edinburgh University Press, 1997).
Best. G , *Mid-Victorian Britain 1851–70* (Glasgow: Fontana, 1982).
Blake, R., *Jardine Matheson: Traders of the Far East* (London: Weidenfeld and Nicolson, 1999).
Bonner-Smith, D. and W. W. R. Lumby (eds), *The Second China War 1856–1860* (London: Navy Records Society, 1954).
Bright, J., *Speeches on Questions of Public Policy*, ed. James E. Thorold Rogers, 2 vols (London: Macmillan, 1869).
Buckle, H. T., *History of Civilization in England*, Volume 1 (London: Parker, 1861).
Bullock, A., and M. Shock, *The Liberal Tradition: From Fox to Keynes* (London: A. and C. Black, 1956).
Burke, E., *Writings and Speeches of Edmund Burke*, Volume 5, ed. P. J. Marshall (Oxford: Clarendon, 1981).

143

Burrow, J. W., *Whigs and Liberals: Continuity and Change in English Political Thought* (Oxford: Clarendon, 1988).

Carlyle, T., *The French Revolution: A History* [1837] (London: Chapman & Hall, 1891).

Carlyle, T., *On Heroes and Hero-Worship* [1841] (London: Oxford University Press, 1974).

Clarke, J. J., *Oriental Enlightenment: The Encounter between Asian and Western Thought* (London: Routledge, 1997).

Condorcet, M. de, *Outlines of an Historical View of the Progress of the Human Mind* (London: J. Johnson, 1795).

Constant, B., *Political Writings*, ed. B. Fontana (Cambridge: Cambridge University Press, 1988).

Dawson, R. (ed.), *The Legacy of China* (Oxford: Clarendon Press, 1964).

Dicey, A. V., *Law and Opinion in England during the Nineteenth Century* [1905] (London: Macmillan, 1963).

Drescher, S., *Dilemmas of Democracy: Tocqueville and Modernization* (Pittsburgh, PA: University of Pittsburgh Press , 1968).

Elias, N., *The Civilizing Process*, Volume 1, *The History of Manners* [1939] (Oxford: Blackwell, 1978).

——, *The Court Society* (New York: Pantheon Books, 1983).

Evans, E. J., *The Forging of the Modern State. Early Industrial Britain 1783–1870* (London: Longman, 1983).

Farrington, A., *Trading Places: The East India Company and Asia 1600–1834* (London: The British Library, 2002).

Ferguson, A., *An Essay on the History of Civil Society* [1767] (Cambridge: Cambridge University Press, 1995).

Forbes, D., 'James Mill and India', *Cambridge Journal*, V, 1951–52, pp. 19–33.

Gobineau, A. de, *Gobineau: Selected Political Writings*, ed. M. D. Biddis (London: Cape, 1970).

Gray, J., *Liberalism*, 2nd edn (Open University Press: Buckingham, 1995).

Greenleaf, W. H., *The British Political Tradition*, Volume 2, *The Ideological Heritage* (London: Routledge, 1988).

Guizot, F., *The History of Civilization in Europe* [1828] (Harmondsworth: Penguin Books, 1997).

Halévy, E., *The Growth of Philosophic Radicalism* (London: Faber and Faber, 1948).

Hampsher-Monk, I., *The Political Philosophy of Edmund Burke* (London: Longman, 1987).

Hazard, P., *European Thought in the Eighteenth Century* (Harmondsworth: Penguin Books, 1965).

Headrick, P. R , *The Tools of Empire: Technology and European Imperialism in the Nineteenth Century* (New York: Oxford University Press, 1981).

Hobbes, T., *Leviathan* [1651] (London: Dent, 1962).

Hobsbawm, E. J., *Industry and Empire* (Harmondsworth: Penguin Books, 1969).

Houghton, W. E., *The Victorian Frame of Mind, 1830–1870* (New Haven, CT: Yale University Press, 1985).

Hume, D., *Enquiries Concerning the Human Understanding and Concerning the Principles of Morals* [1751] (Oxford, Clarendon Press, 1966).

Huntington, S. P., *The Clash of Civilizations and the Remaking of World Order* (New York: Touchstone, 1996).

James, L., *Raj. The Making and Unmaking of British India* (London: Little, Brown, 1997).

Kiernan, V. G., *The Lords of Human Kind: European Attitudes to the Outside World in the Imperial Age* (Harmondsworth: Penguin Books, 1972).

Laski, H. J., *The Rise of European Liberalism* (London: Unwin, 1962).

Levin, M., 'Alexis de Tocqueville: Democracy in America', in M. Forsyth, M. Keens-Soper and J. Hoffman (eds), *The Political Classics: Hamilton to Mill* (Oxford: Oxford University Press, 1993), ch. 5.

Locke, J., *Two Treatises of Government*, intro. P. Laslett [1690] (New York: Mentor, 1965).

Macpherson, C. B., *The Life and Times of Liberal Democracy* (Oxford: Oxford University Press, 1977).

Magnus, P., *Gladstone. A Biography* (London: John Murray, 1963).

Maine, Sir H., *Ancient Law* [1861] (London: Dent, 1954).

Malthus, T., *An Essay on the Principle of Population* [1798] (Harmondsworth: Penguin Books, 1970).

Marshall P. J. and G. Williams, *The Great Map of Mankind: British Perceptions of the World in the Age of Enlightenment* (London: Dent, 1982).

Marx, K. and F. Engels, *Articles on Britain* (Moscow: Progress Publishers, 1975).

Marx Engels Selected Works (London: Lawrence and Wishart, 1962).

Marx Engels Collected Works, Volumes 6, 16, 19 (London: Lawrence and Wishart, 1976, 1980, 1984)

Meek, R. L., 'The Scottish Contribution to Marxist Sociology', in J. Saville (ed.) *Democracy and the Labour Movement* (London: Lawrence and Wishart, 1954), ch. 3.

Mehta, U. S., *Liberalism and Empire: A Study in Nineteenth-Century British Liberal Thought* (Chicago, IL: University of Chicago Press, 1999).

Metcalf, T. R., *Ideologies of the Raj* (Cambridge: Cambridge University Press, 1994).

Mill, James, *The History of British India* (London: James Madden, 1840).

——, *Three Articles from the Encyclopaedia Britannica* (London: J. Innes, 1824).

——, 'Review of "Voyages à Peking, Manille, et l'Ile de France, faits dans l'Intervalle des Années 1784 à 1801" by M. De Guignes', *The Edinburgh Review*, July 1809, Volume 14, pp. 407–29.
——, *Political Writings*, ed. T. Ball (Cambridge: Cambridge University Press, 1992).
Mommsen, W. J., 'Wandlungen der Liberalen Idee im Zeitalter des Imperialismus', in K. Holl and G. List (eds), *Liberalismus und Imperialistischer Staat* (Göttingen: Vandenhoeck and Ruprecht, 1975).
Montesquieu, *The Spirit of the Laws* [1748] (Cambridge: Cambridge University Press, 1989).
Moore, B., Jr, *Social Origins of Dictatorship and Democracy: Lord and Peasant in the Making of the Modern World* (Harmondsworth: Penguin Books, 1969).
Nehru, J., *The Discovery of India*, ed. R. I. Crane (New York: Doubleday, 1959).
Newsinger, J., 'Elgin in China', *New Left Review*, 2nd series, 15, May–June 2002, pp. 119–40.
Parekh, B. (ed.), *Bentham's Political Thought* (London: Croom Helm, 1973).
——, *J. Bentham: Critical Assessments*, 4 vols (London: Routledge, 1993).
Plamenatz, J., *The English Utilitarians* (Oxford: Blackwell, 1949).
Porter, R., *Enlightenment: Britain and the Creation of the Modern World* (Harmondsworth: Penguin Books, 2001).
Rousseau, J.-J., *The Social Contract* [1762] (Harmondsworth: Penguin Books, 1968).
——, *The Social Contract. Discourses*, ed. G. D. H. Cole (London: Dent, 1961).
Said, E. W., *Orientalism: Western Conceptions of the Orient* (Harmondsworth: Penguin Books, 1991).
Sarmiento, D., *Life in the Argentine Republic in the Days of the Tyrants; or, Civilization and Barbarism* [1845] (New York: Hafner, n.d.).
Schlegel, F. von, *The Philosophy of History* [1828] (London: Bohn, 1846).
Smith, A., *The Theory of Moral Sentiments* [1759] (Indianapolis, IN: Liberty Fund, 1984).
——, *The Wealth of Nations* [1776] (Harmondsworth: Penguin Books, 1973).
Spence, Jonathan D., *The Chan's Great Continent: China in Western Minds* (New York: Norton, 1998).
Stokes, E., *The English Utilitarians and India* (Delhi: Oxford University Press, 1992).
Thornton, A. M., 'Philosophic Radicals: Their Influence on Emigration and the Evolution of Responsible Government for the Colonies', in B. Parekh (ed.), *J. Bentham: Critical Assessments*, Volume 4, pp. 332–63.

Thornton, A. P., *Doctrines of Imperialism* (New York: Wiley, 1965).

Thorold Rogers, J. E., (ed.), *Speeches on Questions of Public Policy by John Bright, M.P.* (London: Macmillan, 1869).

Tocqueville, A. de, *Democracy in America*, 2 vols [1835, 1840] (New York: Vintage Books, 1945).

Voltaire, *Voltaire: The Age of Louis XIV and Other Selected Writings*, ed. J. H. Brumfitt (London: New English Library, 1966).

Walker, A., *Marx. His Theory and Its Context* (London: Longman, 1978).

Williams, R., 'Civilization', in *Keywords: A Vocabulary of Culture and Society* (Glasgow: Fontana, 1976).

Index

education, 1, 24, 30, 35, 52, 56, 64, 74, 76,
    77, 89–90, 100, 109, 130, 133–4, 136
Egypt, 11, 12, 65, 66, 76, 97, 101
Elias, N., 10, 11
Elizabeth I, 34
Elphinstone, M., 34, 40
Engels, F., 73, 97
England *see* Great Britain
Enlightenment, 5, 6, 16, 27, 67, 69, 75, 106,
    108, 133
Europe, 10, 11, 12, 13, 15, 17, 19, 20, 28, 35,
    47, 66, 77, 81, 94, 96, 100, 101, 108, 110,
    112–13
Eyre, E. J., 56

Ferguson, A., 5, 9, 11, 12, 20, 28, 31, 32, 81,
    83
Fonblanque, A., 14
Fourier, C., 73, 74, 108
France, 4–6, 9, 10, 11, 14, 16, 17, 20, 21, 24,
    25, 56, 74, 88, 90, 91, 121
freedom *see* liberty
Friedman, R., 112, 114

George III, 103
Germany, 6, 11, 12, 20, 21, 24, 28, 32, 74,
    76, 108
Gibbon, E., 11, 82–3
Gladstone, W. E., 103, 104
Gobineau, A.de, 10, 12, 52, 66Goethe, J.W.
    von, 85
Gomperz, T., 122
Grant, C., 34, 42, 95
Gray, J., 110, 125, 127, 136–7, 138
Great Britain, 3, 5, 10, 11, 14–15, 20, 21,
    22–5, 37, 51–2, 55, 72–4, 81, 84–5, 90–1,
    99, 109–10, 121–2, 124
Greece, ancient, 12, 31, 64, 65, 75–7, 82, 83,
    97
Green, T. H., 131
Greenleaf, W. H., 132
Grey, Earl, 15
Grote, G., 16, 65, 76, 77, 107
Guizot, F., 5, 10, 11, 12, 13, 18, 19, 20, 99,
    105–7, 117

Halevy, E., 42, 43
Hamburger, J., 127–8
Hampsher-Monk, I., 83
Hare, T., 116, 117
Hastings, W., 83
Hegel, G. W. F., 18, 96

Helps, A. 72
Herder, J. G. von, 96
Herodotus, 76
Himmelfarb, G., 113, 116
Hobbes, T., 20, 80, 81, 82, 84
Hobhouse, L. T., 131
Hobsbawm, E., 102
Hobson, J. A., 131
Hugo, V., 34
Humboldt, W. von, 70, 100, 108–9
Hume, D., 10, 71, 82–3, 96
Hutton, R. H., 123

imperialism, colonialism, 40, 42–57, 80,
    135–7
India, 12, 17, 32–57, 66, 75, 94, 95, 96, 97,
    124, 135–6
Ireland, 41, 51, 56, 129
Italy, 12, 123

Japan, 95, 103
Jews, 66
Johnson, Dr S., 9
Jones, Sir W., 34

Kienlung, Emperor of China, 103

Lamartine, A. M. L. de, 34
Lammenais, F.-R. de, 34
law 9, 10, 20, 26, 43
liberalism, 1, 2, 7, 15, 44, 50, 52, 56, 62, 71,
    102, 110, 126–37
liberty, 3, 7, 8, 46, 52, 63, 70, 73, 77, 92, 94,
    100, 105, 109, 110, 114, 116, 123, 125,
    127–9, 135
Locke, J., 9, 10, 32, 80–1, 129

Macaulay, T., 11, 84, 135
Maine, Sir H., 67
Maistre, J. de, 34, 87
Malcolm, Sir J., 34, 40
Malthus, T., 72, 86, 96, 133
Marx, K., 1, 6, 20, 52, 62, 66, 68, 69, 70, 73,
    85, 97, 103
mass society, 7, 21, 25, 27, 86–92, 97, 99,
    109–10, 112, 113–15, 127
M'Culloch, J. R., 16
Mehta, U. S., 56, 137
Melbourne, Lord, 23
Metcalf, T. R., 53, 55
Metcalfe, C., 34
Mill, Harriet, 33